STRANGE HILL HIGH

MITCHELL'S GUIDE TO STRANGE HILL HIGH

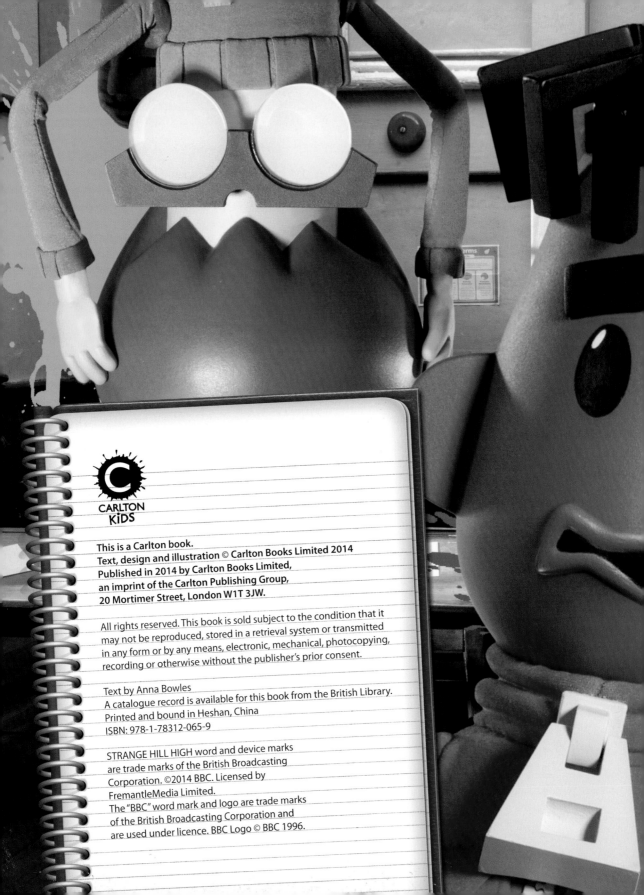

CARLTON KIDS

This is a Carlton book.
Text, design and illustration © Carlton Books Limited 2014
Published in 2014 by Carlton Books Limited,
an imprint of the Carlton Publishing Group,
20 Mortimer Street, London W1T 3JW.

Text by Anna Bowles
A catalogue record is available for this book from the British Library.
Printed and bound in Heshan, China
ISBN: 978-1-78312-065-9

MITCHELL'S GUIDE TO STRANGE HILL HIGH

CHAOS!

CRINGING!

TOILETS!

TENTACLES!

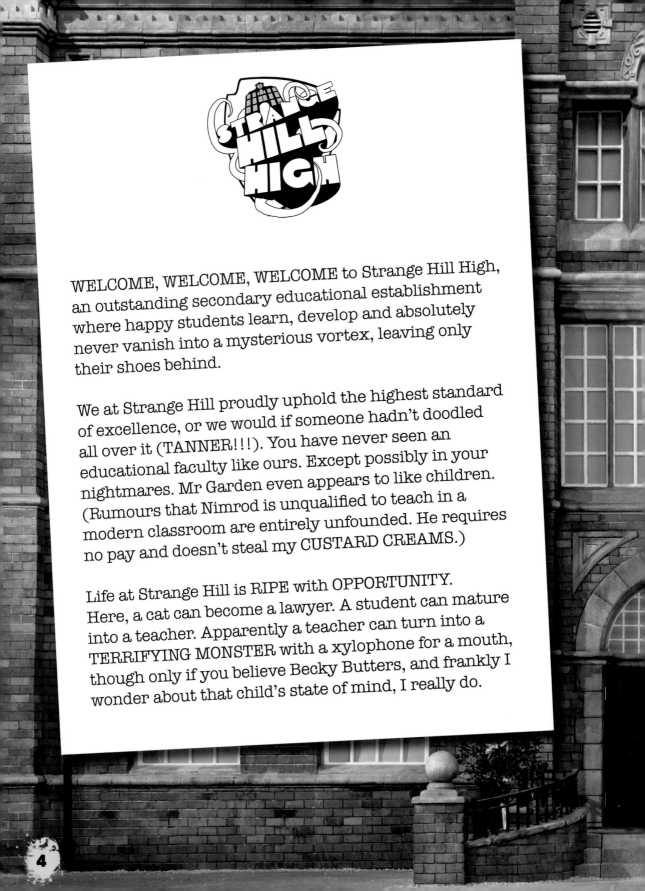

WELCOME, WELCOME, WELCOME to Strange Hill High, an outstanding secondary educational establishment where happy students learn, develop and absolutely never vanish into a mysterious vortex, leaving only their shoes behind.

We at Strange Hill proudly uphold the highest standard of excellence, or we would if someone hadn't doodled all over it (TANNER!!!). You have never seen an educational faculty like ours. Except possibly in your nightmares. Mr Garden even appears to like children. (Rumours that Nimrod is unqualified to teach in a modern classroom are entirely unfounded. He requires no pay and doesn't steal my CUSTARD CREAMS.)

Life at Strange Hill is RIPE with OPPORTUNITY. Here, a cat can become a lawyer. A student can mature into a teacher. Apparently a teacher can turn into a TERRIFYING MONSTER with a xylophone for a mouth, though only if you believe Becky Butters, and frankly I wonder about that child's state of mind, I really do.

On the pastoral side, my team and I are dedicated to student welfare. In particular I find that students fare very well a long, long way away from me while I enjoy a nice cup of tea and a biscuit. Parents are also invited not to STICK THEIR NOSES into the running of the school, because teachers are always RIGHT.

In conclusion, I am delighted to welcome you into the Strange Hill family. It is my fervent hope that you survive the next seven years, or at any rate that you don't blame me when something EATS YOU.

Yours extremely sincerely,

Abercrombie

Melvyn Abercrombie
BA (Honest),
Basingstoke Stereo Salesmen's College

P.S. Students scheduled for lessons with Mr Dougherty should apply to the school nurse for the full range of vaccinations.

WHASSUP?

SO YOU'RE STUCK AT THIS PLACE TOO, AM I RIGHT?
At least I'm not the new boy any more, then. It's probably,
like, my duty to help you survive. That's where this book comes
in (Duty's not my bag, so you read this and I'll just chill)

Anyway, at Strange Hill you've got to watch out for
teachers, bullies, horrible food, PE lessons... oh yeah,
and monsters and ghosts and stuff. IT GETS PRETTY
WEIRD. And when you get transported to a strange
dimension where you have to battle horrible creatures,
you STILL don't get let off homework. It's harsh.

The important thing is to have a positive attitude,
and remember there's no situation so bad that a really
GOOD EXCUSE can't at least confuse the teacher so
much they BLOW A CIRCUIT (works on Nimrod, anyway).
Stand by your friends, and they'll stand by you, though
if Templeton's involved you should watch out for him
mistaking you for KING OF THE MARTIANS and
trying to burn offerings on your shoes.

When the WEIRD STUFF happens, us kids are usually in it on our own. Teachers run screaming, though I guess they might stick around if there was a biscuit in it for them – I might try that next time I actually need a teacher, ie. never.

Most of all... most of all... well, don't ask me. I just like to take it easy and not have to save the world more than twice a week. So let's just HANG OUT AND CHILL, yeah?

Mitchell

Stephanie Bethany

Samia Speed

STUDENT PROFILES

Bishop

Croydonia Puttock

Matthews

Gazza Taggit

8

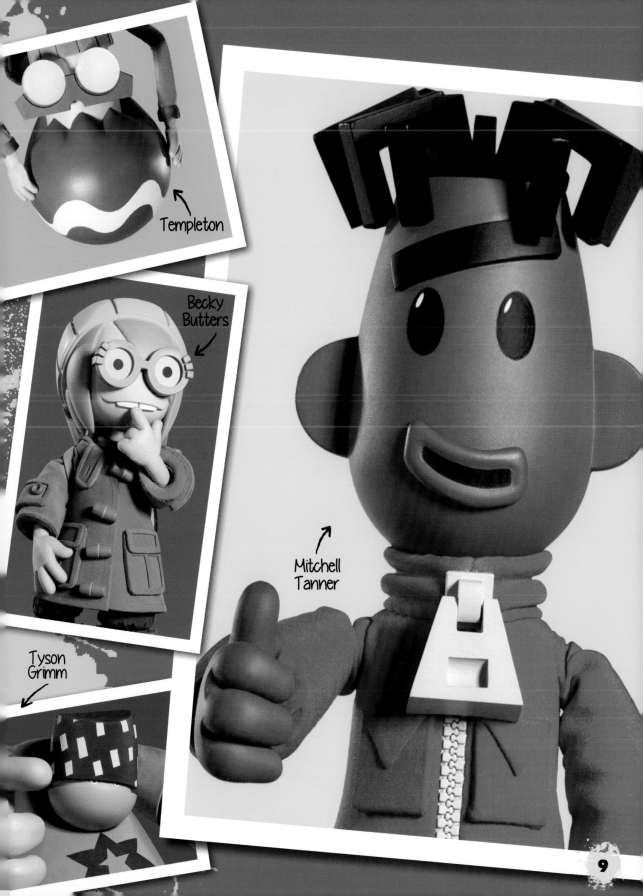

Templeton

Becky
Butters

Tyson
Grimm

Mitchell
Tanner

MITCHELL TANNER

MEET MITCHELL

Mitchell Tanner is without doubt the GREATEST HERO Strange Hill High or possibly the world has ever seen!

He's got a yoyo, he beatboxes, he skateboards, he battles giant mutated school pets and he gets bad grades. He's cool. Me and Templeton have been his best friends ever since he started at Strange Hill. He's saved us from an EVIL, TENTACLED TOILET MONSTER and a psychotic tooth fairy.

WHAT'S IN A NAME?

Mitchell's middle name is Jojo. He copes pretty well with the psychological scarring this must have caused.

WHAT'S . . . WHAT?

Mitchell's ATTENTION SPAN is about five seconds. Luckily he comes back to important stuff in the end, he just goes the long way around.

GOOD POINTS

- Mitchell's very loyal to his best friends. Even when Templeton is stranger than usual.
- He's really relaxed and chilled. I don't think I really worry too much but I do worry sometimes, and he doesn't.
- He always saves the day. Usually by doing something that's COMPLETELY NUTS, but it works out somehow.

BECKY BUTTERS

MEET BECKY

Becky is the sensitive, creative one around here. A bit too sensitive maybe, because sometimes if you say something that's true, like how her singing is not quite... well yeah. It's best not to say that sort of thing.

She cares about people and animals and healthy eating and probably about DEPRIVED HOMELESS BACTERIA as well. She loves gardening and grew Mr Creeper, which goes to show that enthusiasm is not always a good idea

PET PRINCESS

Becky loves "ickle-wickle itsy-witsy cutesy" animals, and coos over them. At least we hope that's what she's doing, not summoning the Dark Lord in some ancient lingo.

QUEEN OF SELF-ESTEEM

Becky has a list of affirmations stuck inside her locker, such as "I love and approve of myself" and "I am peaceful with life". Once I added "I do Mitchell's homework" to the list – but she spotted it!

GOOD POINTS

* Becks is uptight, which is actually cool because she can use all that energy to do my science project
* She eats all that fruit and vegetable stuff that's supposed to make you healthy. Someone's gotta do it.
* Becky's excellent at pointing out if an idea will totally backfire.

> Becky is MAJORLY ENTHUSIASTIC.

TEMPLETON

MEET TEMPLETON

Some say Templeton landed on Earth during a meteor shower from the planet Baloney. Others reckon he was raised in the wild by disused ARTIFICIALLY INTELLIGENT CHOCOLATE VENDING MACHINES.

One thing's for sure. Templeton is most definitely... TEMPLETONY.

Whatever happens, in reality he always has a weird alternative theory. Which is almost always WRONG.

When we have adventures, he's like a magnet for mishap. And he insists on worshipping everything. He makes Strange Hill even stranger.

> I heard he was found down the back of his aunt Ethel's sofa!

SOCK STYLE

Style isn't Templeton's strong suit, but at least you can always see him coming. Peter Dustpan called him a "beautiful poodle boy", whatever one of those is.

WHAT'S UP?

Whatever's happening, Templeton thinks something else is happening. Something EVEN WEIRDER, which given the normal level of weirdness round here, is pretty impressive.

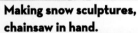

Making snow sculptures, chainsaw in hand.

GOOD POINTS

* Looks really scientific in a lab coat.
* Makes great snow sculptures with a chainsaw.
* Comes up with ideas so daft that even Mitchell's ideas look clever in comparison.

Stephanie Bethany

EWWW! That's what Stephanie Bethany thinks of you, and of everyone else except her BFF Croydonia. She's so cool she wouldn't even notice your tragic existence. Luckily you don't want her to notice you because she's **RUDE, SNOTTY, STUCK-UP, SMUG,** and did we mention **RUDE?**

Stephanie Bethany (nobody knows if "Bethany" is her surname or what) gets elected class president every year because everybody likes her. Or at any rate they know that if they admit they don't like her they'll become complete **SOCIAL OUTCASTS** forever.

Stephanie ropes Bocky into her election campaign.

16

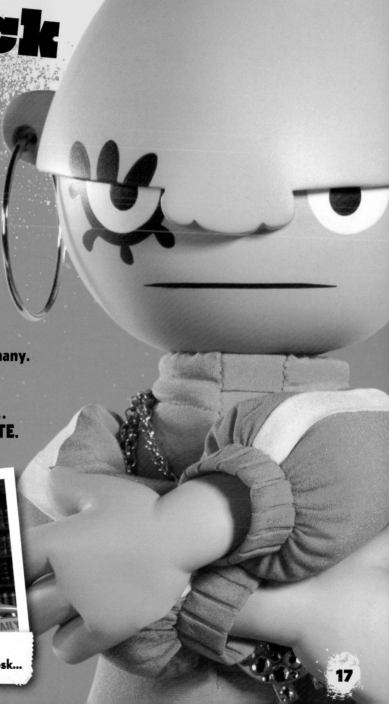

Croydonia Puttock

Croydonia is **TOTES SOPHISTICATED**. It's the kind of sophistication you pick up hanging round a fried chicken shop after school on a Friday. She's sassy, confident and **WAAAAY LESS CLEVER** than she thinks. But as editor of *The Daily Weekly* she wields some serious power in the school, and she's best mates with Queen of Flipping Everything, Stephanie Bethany.

So if you want to know what's really cool, ask Croydonia Puttock… and then do the **EXACT OPPOSITE**.

Croydonia on the "Daily Weekly" desk…

Tyson Grimm, Lucas Montgomery and Bishop

What's not to love about these three CHARMING SCALLYWAGS? Well, actually, let's see, there's Bishop's tragic bling obsession, Tyson's THUGGISHNESS, Lucas' delusion that he's some kind of Bond villain... yeah.

LUCAS MONTGOMERY

Lucas is the LEADER OF THE GANG, with his red wraparound shades, sinister snigger and relatively functional brain. It's a pity he thinks that telling Miss Grackle that the Strange Hill teachers send him to sleep is the pinnacle of daring humour. In his dreams, he's as cool as Mitchell. In reality he's as LUKEWARM AS THE COOK'S HOTDOG GHOULASH.

BISHOP

YO! WHASSUP? The third of the trio, Bling King Bishop, lacks both brains and brawn, but he does have a really, really **BIG MEDALLION.** And a permanent cast on his forearm, for some unknown reason. Bishop is a bit less hostile than the other two, and in an emergency, he sometimes helps out Mitchell and co. Just don't expect him to admit it afterwards.

TYSON GRIMM

What Tyson lacks in intelligence… Tyson also lacks in most other areas. He's basically just good at **THUMPING PEOPLE** and nicking their stuff. At least he knows his limitations, and generally declines to get too involved if thinking's on the cards.

19

Samia Speed

Samia has one of the **SHARPEST MINDS AT STRANGE HILL,** even if her speaking device delivers everything in a deadpan tone. She doesn't miss much, especially opportunities to charge Mitchell fees for everything from using her wheelchair as a taxi to hacking the school database. **GOTHIC CHIC** is Samia's signature style. She has the world's cutest **MINI-SKULLS** tying her bunches, and a couple more on her wheels. While Stephanie's cutesiness is actually anything but friendly, Samia's **OBSERVANT PATIENCE** makes her a useful friend.

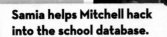

Samia helps Mitchell hack into the school database.

Matthews

Matthews is **HAPPY**. Nobody knows why, and nobody knows how, considering he's at Strange Hill High and has to deal with ghosts, monsters and Abercrombie on a daily basis. Being shoved head-down in a bin, winning the lottery and getting stuck to his chair with chewing gum all provoke **SHINY-TOOTHED DELIGHT** in Matthews. Only in extreme circumstances, such as when the library is mentioned, does he take time out for a spot of raving panic. It's possible there's something **TERRIBLY WRONG** with Matthews... but that would just make him normal around here.

Matthews has a permanent grin on his face for some strange reason.

Miko and Mikiko

CUTE! And funny! And **FULL OF SWEETS!** That's how Miko and Mikiko like things to be, and usually how they are themselves. The Japanese-born twins agree on everything, and they generally agree that they **LOVE IT.** Miko is the one with the red bow that has white spots, and Mikiko is the one with the white bow that has red spots... except they're quite capable of pretending to be each other for a **TRICK,** so who knows?

In "The 101 % Solution", the twins even turn into a trio!

GAZZA TAGGIT

Junior anarchist Gazza Taggit is a **BOY OF FEW WORDS.** None at all, in fact, unless you count words that are **SPRAY-PAINTED ON WALLS.** He has a lot of those, all over the school. Miss Grimshaw's CCTV system is on **PERMANENT ALERT** for him.

Taggit doing what he does best on the school walls.

Donald

The **UNLUCKIEST BOY IN THE SCHOOL,** Donald looks permanently alarmed for good reason. If there's an evil book just waiting to swallow readers into a time vortex, you can bet he reads it. Strange Hill is a difficult place, and Donald has a **DIFFICULT TIME,** and you should basically just be thankful you **AREN'T HIM.**

23

Miss Grimshaw

Mr Creeper

The Libra[ry]

TEACHER PROFILES

Mr Garden

Mr Balding

Miss Grackle

Mr Abercrombie

The Cook

Nimrod

Mr Abercrombie

Abercrombie is a **VISIONARY HEADMASTER**, respected by staff and students alike for his intellect, leadership skills and collection of **PINKY PONIES**. Well… one of those things is true. Half-true, anyway. He does have a collection of Pinky Ponies. Abercrombie runs a tight ship at Strange Hill High, with advanced security systems, **RIGID DISCIPLINE** and absolutely no tolerance of students' ridiculous stories about monsters, even when the monsters are actually **TRASHING THE PLACE.** He came 103rd among the 106 students in his year at Basingstoke Stereo Salesman College, a fact which he seems to think proves something. Who knows what?

In "Innercrombie", the kids get inside Abercrombie's head and cause havoc!

Miss Grimshaw

Everyone needs to find something they enjoy, and the pleasure in School Secretary Miss Daisy Mae Grimshaw's life comes from shouting **"NO RUNNING"** at children from behind the window of the school office. Not that she has a limited range of interests: she also enjoys using the tannoy system to **SHOUT AT LATECOMERS**, making people fill in forms, tutting in irritation and **GLARING**. Strange Hill High is the ideal environment for all these activities, so it seems likely that Miss Grimshaw has found true happiness. Just don't expect her to cause it in anyone else.

Miss Grimshaw searches Mitchell's locker for things that have gone missing.

Mr Balding

Bartleby Balding is the most **BORING IMMORTAL HISTORY TEACHER** in the history of boring immortal history teachers. Actually that may not be hard, because only at Strange Hill could immortality seem like a minor detail. But he's also probably the **MOST BORING HISTORY TEACHER** in the history of all history teachers. That's way harder to achieve. He's so boring that his book about Strange Hill opened a **BOREHOLE IN TIME** and… yeah, this is probably boring you. Oh, and he's also that old guy with the big belly who goes "Ho, ho, ho!" But he doesn't seem to talk about that. Maybe he thinks it's **BORING**.

Mr Balding was teaching at Strange Hill High back in 1881!

The Librarian

The Librarian (AKA The lady) (real name unknown: rumour has it that she **SACRIFICED IT TO A WORD-EATING MANUSCRIPT** in exchange for her **BOOK-KWON-DO POWERZ**) would be absolutely terrifying were it not that she's at Strange Hill, where she fits in nicely. She hates children so much that she'd rather see them sucked into a **BOREHOLE** than roaming her library **WIPING BOGEYS** on Henry Wadsworth Longfellow. Possibly the most terrifying thing about her is that she seems to harbour a secret affection for the Headmaster, which is revealed in "Innercrombie". She has a favourite love poem, too.

The Librarian photocopies Mitchell's head!

Miss Grackle

Miss Grackle still lives at home **WITH HER MOTHER** and resents it almost as much as the fact that she has to teach music to a load of **TIN-EARED KIDS.**

Mr Creeper

Slave-driving Mr Creeper is a **SENTIENT PLANT** who wants kids to breathe out loads of carbon dioxide that will enable his kind to spread across the world. He's almost as bad as the **PE TEACHERS AT YOUR SCHOOL.**

Mr Garden

Mr Garden likes kids and wants to HELP them. YOUNG AND IDEALISTIC, he got into teaching in order to inspire children with a love of literature. This is pretty weird, but there's no sign (yet) that he's an alien/robot/spy.

Mr Kandinsky

To be taught by the passionate Mr Kandinsky is to feel your INNER CREATIVITY BLOSSOM, or possibly solidify into a TERRIFYING CLAY CREATURE if you're Templeton. But if you make a mess Mr Kandinsky will still give you an "F".

Murdoch

Caretaker or **TRASH PIRATE?** Murdoch is both. He's got cleaning fluid in his blood (Ouch! Call the school nurse...) and he's just as happy **SWEET-TALKING GENNY THE GENERATOR** as launching plunger harpoons from the school roof. Just so long as he doesn't actually have to repair anything.

Mr Doughert

SAVAGE – but surprisingly friendly – Deputy Head Mr Dougherty is kept chained up on the forbidden fourth floor for the safety of all concerned. For one bite from this **RAGGED MAN** will turn you into the most dreadful of all monsters, a **WERE-TEACHER**.

Nimrod

Supercomputer, war machine, big bleepy bore… Maths teacher Nimrod was once the **MOST POWERFUL PROCESSING DEVICE** on the planet, and he doesn't even need coffee breaks. Of course, that was 60 years ago. Now he's clapped out and frequently **ON THE BLINK**. But he still skips the coffee.

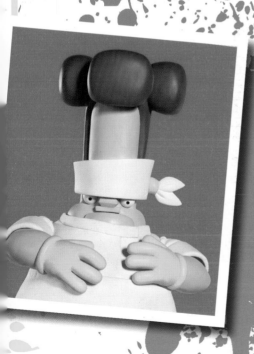

The Cook

What's important about school food? Taste? Nutrition? Hygiene? Nah, try cheapness and convenience. For Cook, if it's **PAST ITS SELL-BY DATE**, it's a bargain, and if you can make it by getting the monster of the week to smush up potatoes then that's a handy time saving. **MOULDY NUGGETS** and limp chips coming up!

The Ghost Children

The Embarrassment

GUEST CHARACTERS

Safety Toad

Rapscallion

Templeton Alien

Miss Cate

Ken Kong

The Tooth Fairy

The Grackle

Miss Joy

The Tooth Fairy

Quake at the evil of the Tooth Fairy! Yes, go on – **QUAKE WITH LAUGHTER**. Because he is kind of evil, sure, but the voice? And the **DRESS SENSE**? Mm. It's hard not to feel a tiny bit sorry for him. The Tooth Fairy's Smilophone – now that's scary.

The Grackle

The Grackle is a **PROPER SCARY MONSTER**, made out of bits of Becky's nightmares. She can be defeated by nice singing, which is a bit **CHEESY**, but not as cheesy as trying to rhyme "Grackle" with "dental plaquele".

Miss Cate

Miss Cate is lovely and kind and nice and understanding and turns out to be part of a **SINISTER ROBOT CONSPIRACY** to impose order on the world by brainwashing everyone. At least things will be clean and efficient when she's in charge.

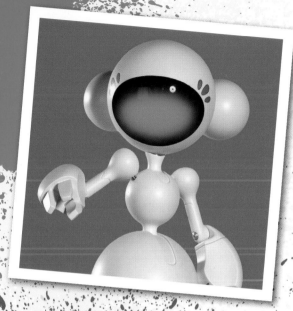

Peter Dustpan

Peter Dustpan was abandoned by his parents a hundred years ago. Since then he's **LIVED ALONE IN THE LOST AND FOUND CUPBOARD,** playing and playing and playing. The only thing he's missing is some friends… and his **MARBLES.** Would you like to be this boy's special chum?

Sir Bogivere

The most noble knight Sir Bogivere has been tasked with **GUARDING THE FOUL LATRINE FOR ETERNITY**, lest **HE WHO CANNOT BE FLUSHED** return to plague the world. Luckily he's very antisocial so he's quite happy in there.

Bocky

You know Becky is enthusiastic, kind and insecure? Well, clay Becky statue Bocky is **ENTHUSIASTIC!! KIND!!!** and **INSECURE!!!** Plus a tiny bit gullible, which is how she ends up in league with Stephanie. But she proves her heart is as big as Becky's when she sacrifices herself to defend her friend.

Safety Toad

The Safety Toad is **A KIND OF IMAGINARY FRIEND** invented by Becky when she was little. He's big on mellowness, and getting through crises without panicking. Unfortunately if that doesn't work he's **UTTERLY USELESS.**

Ghost Children

The Ghost Children haunt the **DETENTION OF THE CURSED,** from which they shall never be released. They were briefly exploited by Mitchell as a **HOMEWORK FACTORY,** but now they're making hipster hats for Abercrombie.

Mr Tanner

What could make Mitchell uncool? NOTHING, RIGHT? Except for the slow and terrible passage of years, destroying his hopes and dreams. Yes, GRUMPY, POT-BELLIED DISCIPLINARIAN Mr Tanner is a chilling vision of Mitchell's possible future. Think about how YOU would look as a teacher... and be very afraid.

Ian Gatlurn

Ian Gatlurn was a 1950s MATHS GENIUS who was frozen waiting for "the future". Defrosted after his use by date he's gone a BIT NUTZ and lost his head..., literally as Mitchell accidentally chipped it off. Now he's OBSESSED WITH THE WONDERS OF GEOGRAPHY. And has a glorious future in stew.

The G-Man

The G-Man, aka Agent Vector from the Ministry of Applied Mathematics, has come to save the world from Mitchell's destruction of maths. His method? Burying the school in concrete and TAKING MITCHELL'S BRAIN TO STICK IN A JAR? Some think this is too extreme.

The Templeton Aliens

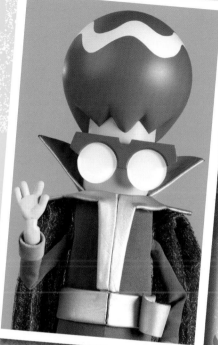

They all look like Templeton. **THEY ALL WANT TO EAT TEMPLETON,** because nothing else in the universe is Templetony enough. This makes no sense, except that by Templetonian standards it's really no weirder than most things. **PASS THE KETCHUP!**

Ken Kong

Ken Kong is an ordinary boy with a Mitchell-esque **LOVE OF LAZING ABOUT.** He just happens to be 100 feet tall as a result of eating giant fruit. Oh well, that's life. Hopefully he walked home to Mongolia without **FLATTENING HALF OF EUROPE.**

The Embarrassment

Michael Barrisment was a student obsessed with **PRANKING ABERCROMBIE,** until he spent 25 years in ultra-detention. **WARPED AND FESTERING IN HIS OWN SHAME,** he emerged as The Embarrassment, bent on embarrassing everyone on Earth from his HQ in the school gym. Well, everyone needs a project.

Rapscallion

The Knavish Rapscallion, currently inhabiting the body of one Melvyn Abercrombie, is the sworn foe of **YE OLDE RIGHTEOUSNESS LEAGUE.** He's also a **DAB HAND WITH NAFF TWEETS,** and other terrible weapons that will enable him to steal the world's technology if not stopped by Mitchell and co.

Mitchell Junior

EVIL, OBSESSED WITH CHOCOLATE...
no it's not actually Abercrombie but the
terrifying Mitchell Junior, a Victorian doll
intended to teach kids about responsibility
and taking care of others. Instead it takes care
of all the other dolls by **DESTROYING** them.

Miss Joy

Miss Joy, otherwise known as Terpsichore,
is a goddess who wants to open a portal
between her world and ours so that
everyone can live in harmony and **SING
AND DANCE FOREVER.** Very nice, unless
you're Mitchell; she needs to **SACRIFICE**
him to pull off her plan.

SCHOOL LIFE

The Library... it's not all that it seems...

Weird things happen in this Clock Tower.

Where all the action takes place...

45

Places to be ~~Educated~~ ~~Bored~~ Terrified

The School Entrance

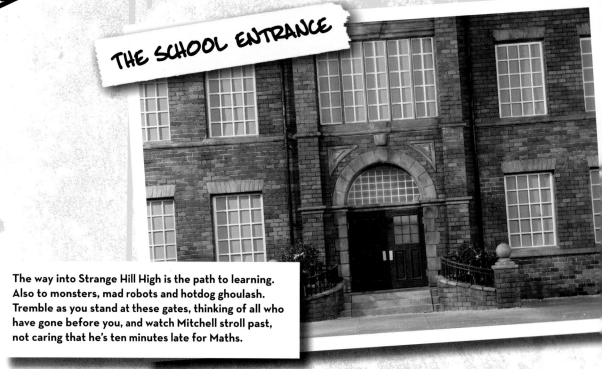

The way into Strange Hill High is the path to learning. Also to monsters, mad robots and hotdog ghoulash. Tremble as you stand at these gates, thinking of all who have gone before you, and watch Mitchell stroll past, not caring that he's ten minutes late for Maths.

The Corridor

The scuffed floorboards, the worn-out lockers, the cabbage-green paint... it's like it was built to order by Dingy Schools R Us. Actually it was built to order by the amazing Strange Hill props department, but isn't it chillingly perfect?

THE LIBRARY

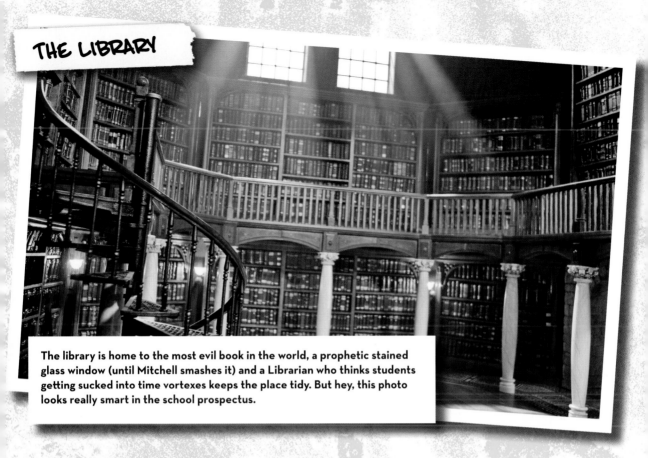

The library is home to the most evil book in the world, a prophetic stained glass window (until Mitchell smashes it) and a Librarian who thinks students getting sucked into time vortexes keeps the place tidy. But hey, this photo looks really smart in the school prospectus.

THE CLASSROOM

In rooms like these, the true business of Strange Hill is conducted. Does that mean education? Nah, it's yoyo tournaments, texting, swapsies, etc.

THE CLOCK TOWER

The **Strange Hill clock tower** is just like any other, apart from the fact that it houses weird machinery that can send you backwards or forwards in time. Just not very far backwards or forwards, unless you crank the handle a lot.

THE FOUL LATRINE

Behold the Foul Latrine! Tremble at the name of He Who Cannot be Flushed! And avoid toilet guardian Sir Bogivere, because he's rather antisocial.

THE KITCHEN

The kitchen of Strange Hill High is full of out-of-date chicken nuggets, wilted veg and additive stew. And we'd better hope it stays that way, because if Cook runs out he'll probably start serving up bits of the various monsters that Mitchell and co have seen off.

MR ABERCROMBIE'S OFFICE

Mr Abercrombie's office is a refuge for the hardworking headmaster, where he can scoff insanity bars, play with his Pinky Ponies, plot mass detentions and generally lurk.

HOMEWORK HELP

Stuck with your homework? What you should do is ask one of the geniuses of Strange Hill to help you. Here are some examples. Why not hand them in as your own work and admire the beautiful "F" your teacher writes at the bottom?

MITCHELL

HISTORY

WHAT HAPPENED AT 1066?

At 10.66 right, we realized something had been messing with the clocks. It was some evil fairy queen, this weird little woman in a doily who wanted to stop us going on break so her army of pink fiends could take over the playground, though who knows what on Earth they'd want our manky playground for. It was drizzling that day...

Mitchell, Mr Balding meant the YEAR 1066!
Becks.

Oh. Well I don't know what happened then, I wasn't there! Baldie probably was, so why's he asking me?

In 1066, Anglo Saxon was defeated by Norman. Norman thought England should belong to him, so he stole it from his mate Anglo by shooting him and his army with arrows made of wood and metal, because guns aren't allowed in England. Norman had been living in France, which my auntie says is a horrible place where they eat funny stuff, so who can blame him, though I think my auntie needs to get out more because we went to Britney for a holiday and it was OK. Maybe French people ate fish and chips in 1066. But we can't be sure, because history was a long, long time ago.

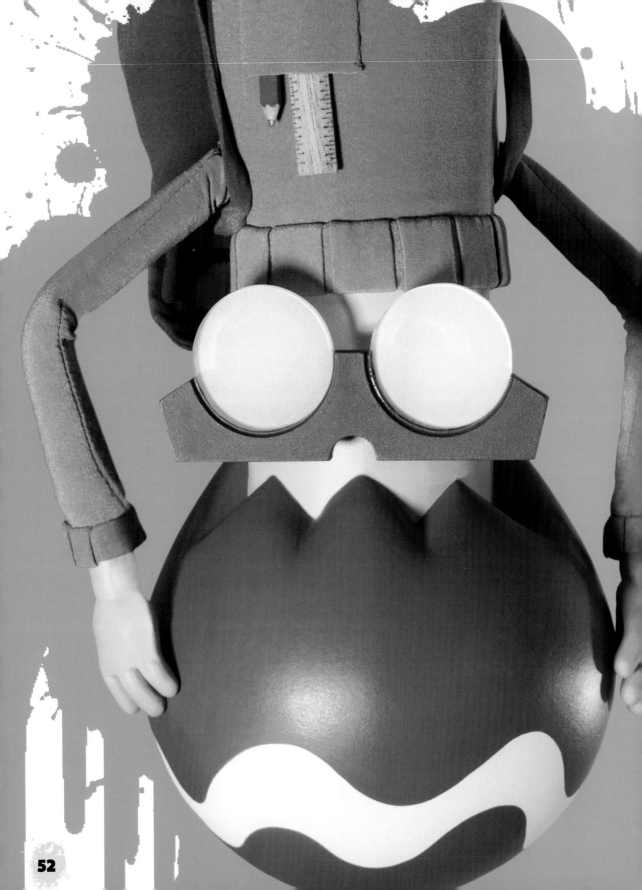

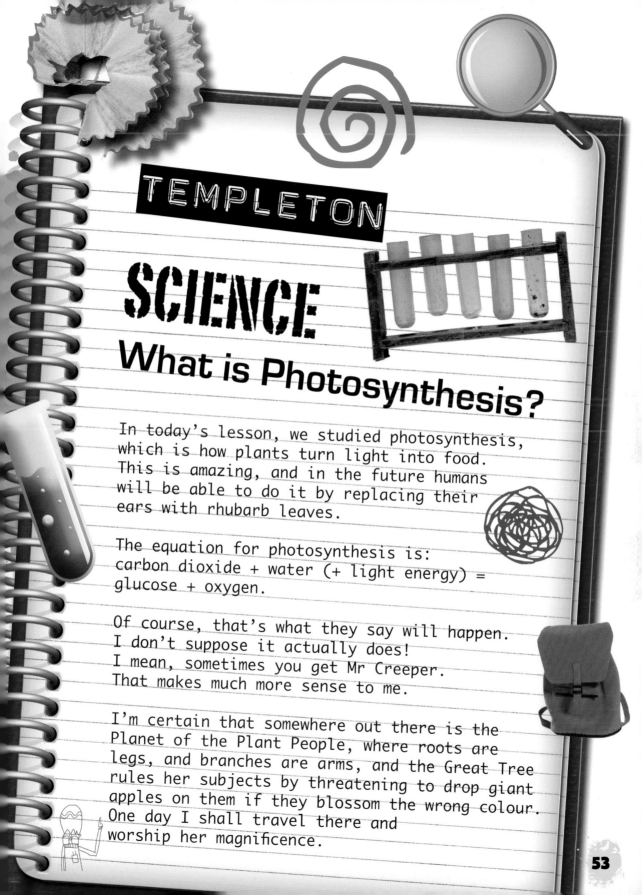

TEMPLETON

SCIENCE

What is Photosynthesis?

In today's lesson, we studied photosynthesis, which is how plants turn light into food. This is amazing, and in the future humans will be able to do it by replacing their ears with rhubarb leaves.

The equation for photosynthesis is: carbon dioxide + water (+ light energy) = glucose + oxygen.

Of course, that's what they say will happen. I don't suppose it actually does! I mean, sometimes you get Mr Creeper. That makes much more sense to me.

I'm certain that somewhere out there is the Planet of the Plant People, where roots are legs, and branches are arms, and the Great Tree rules her subjects by threatening to drop giant apples on them if they blossom the wrong colour. One day I shall travel there and worship her magnificence.

ENGLISH
BOOK REPORT: "THE HOBBIT"

Bilbo the ickle hobbit is so cute, with hair on his toesy-woesies! He meets a bear and a thrush and eagles and a totally adorable dragon who only burns people because they want to steal his bed. (Wouldn't you?)

The theme of the book is friendship, because Bilbo has a lot of friends. They're all boys though and I know how difficult that is. The dwarves really need to establish an eco-collective to keep things going at the Lonely Mountain because they can't eat gold, and also they'll die out without any girls, so it really is time to invite the elves to live there too.

Bilbo faces many dangers and becomes older and wiser by the end of the book, although the dangers aren't actually that dangerous compared to the stuff that goes on every day here. Except we haven't had a dragon. Yet. OK, I've scared myself now.

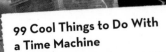

99 Cool Things to Do With a Time Machine

EPISODE GUIDE

SEASON 1

EPISODES 1-14

PAGES 58-85

SEASON 2

EPISODES 1-13

PAGES 86-111

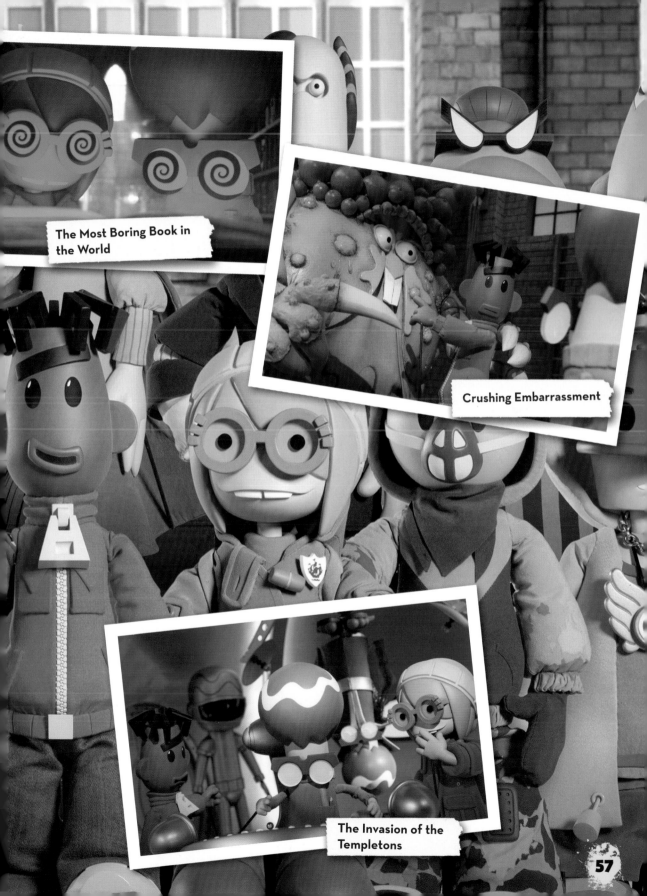

The Most Boring Book in the World

Crushing Embarrassment

The Invasion of the Templetons

57

KING MITCHELL

A freak event at Strange Hill High: Mitchell has done his woodwork homework! Unfortunately the fruits of his labour don't last long. Tyson snatches Mitchell's wooden skateboard, goes flying and cracks his thick head against the wall of the toilet block.

The wall crumbles and reveals... a long-forgotten secret chamber, containing a gigantic toilet and ancient artefacts. Behind dusty cobwebs, Mitchell finds a magnificent round oak table, which he thinks will replace his broken skateboard. What he doesn't know is that this is a mythical table, and by laying claim to it he's unintentionally declared himself "King Mitchell" and unleashed Sir Bogivere, the guardian of the Foul Latrine, from his ancient slumber.

Seeing an armed knight, Mitchell legs it. But Sir Bogivere is not interested in taking vengeance. Instead he goes down on one knee and declares loyalty to "King Mitchell". Mitchell, naturally, exploits this like mad. His weird requests worry the noble knight, who is neglecting his primary duty of protecting the world from the foul pit of eternal evil (the toilet).

When Becky lets slip that Mitchell isn't a real king but just a schoolboy, Bogivere challenges Mitchell to a duel to restore his honour, and to rescue Becky from becoming Bogivere's eternal companion. Swords are so 12th century, so it's scissors, paper, stone to the death... or at least to something a bit nasty.

Sir Bogivere hails Mitchell as his king and master.

While Mitchell and Bogivere battle, the ancient toilet evil attempts to break out of its festering prison. It looks like the world is doomed when Bogivere is snatched by the disgusting tentacles, but Mitchell reaches for "Excalibur", the toilet cleaner of destiny. Only a true King can release the powerful weapon from its bed of dried-on muck!

When Mitchell frees Excalibur he demonstrates his true royal status. The evil is vanquished, Becky is free, and Sir Bogivere returns to his post as guardian while Mitchell returns the round table to its rightful place and reseals the secret chamber.

Now all Mitchell has to worry about is cleaning the toilets before Abercrombie shows up... that and his woodwork homework?!

Mitchell pulls Bogivere free from the tentacles with the help of Excalibur.

Mitchell lifts Excalibur and the toilets are suddenly clean!

99 COOL THINGS TO DO WITH a TIME MACHINE

Mitchell struggles to turn back the clock.

It's exams week at Strange Hill High and if Mitchell is late again, he's going to be in big trouble. Unluckily for him, the school clock is about to chime for the start of school. So Mitchell climbs the precarious school clock tower to put back the hands by 10 minutes (obviously!). No one will ever know. However, when he arrives at class he is 10 minutes early – he has turned back time itself!

Excited, Mitchell shows Becky and Templeton the mechanism in the tower and they have some fun – going back to days with the best school lunch, outwitting teachers, fast-forwarding through boring lessons, slowing down breaktime etc.

Nevertheless, Becky is adamant that however much time they have they still need to study for the exams. But Mitchell reckons he has a better idea. The exam papers are locked in a time-coded vault, which will only open after the exams have happened. If he jumps forward to that time, he can get the answers and take them back to before he sits the exam.

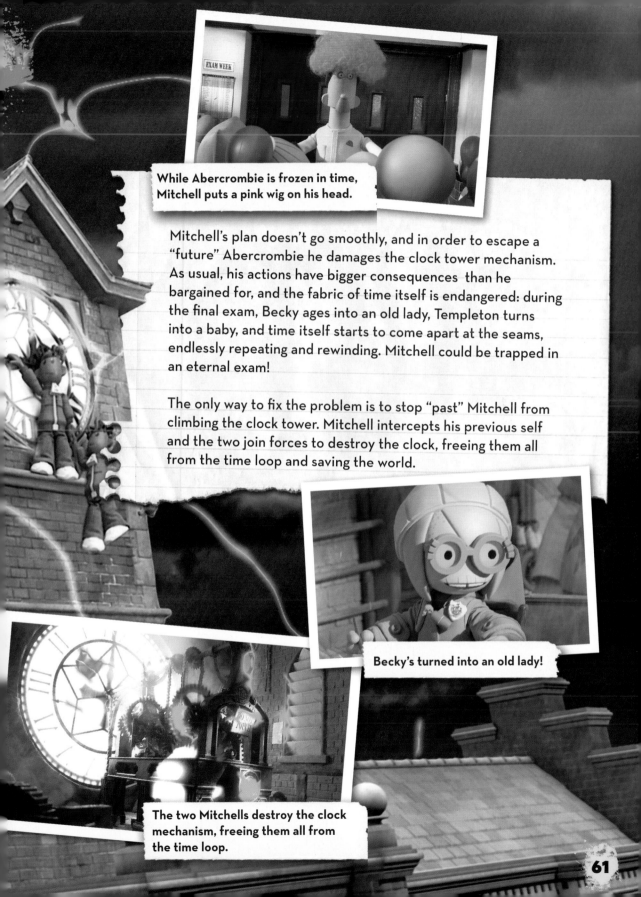

While Abercrombie is frozen in time, Mitchell puts a pink wig on his head.

Mitchell's plan doesn't go smoothly, and in order to escape a "future" Abercrombie he damages the clock tower mechanism. As usual, his actions have bigger consequences than he bargained for, and the fabric of time itself is endangered: during the final exam, Becky ages into an old lady, Templeton turns into a baby, and time itself starts to come apart at the seams, endlessly repeating and rewinding. Mitchell could be trapped in an eternal exam!

The only way to fix the problem is to stop "past" Mitchell from climbing the clock tower. Mitchell intercepts his previous self and the two join forces to destroy the clock, freeing them all from the time loop and saving the world.

Becky's turned into an old lady!

The two Mitchells destroy the clock mechanism, freeing them all from the time loop.

THE LOST AND FOUND BOY

Mitchell, Becky and Templeton explore the dark vaults of the Lost and Found room.

On his way to school, Mitchell meets a strange, old-fashioned man who is looking for his son. Before Mitchell can find out the son's name, the man vanishes. Meanwhile, things are going missing all around school, including Templeton's trousers. New boy Mitchell is identified as prime suspect, and what's worse, incriminating evidence is found in his locker. If Mitchell can't clear his name by finding the missing items, he will be expelled.

Mitchell, Becky and Templeton investigate the obvious place to find missing objects – the Lost and Found room. But far from the tiny cupboard they were expecting, it turns out to be an endless maze of corridors made up of discarded kitten jumpers and hundreds of years of junk. What's more, they're not alone.

"Hello, I'm Peter Dustpan!"

The trio are ambushed by Peter Dustpan, an Edwardian boy who has been hiding in the room for more than 100 years. He was apparently abandoned by his parents, who never came to pick him up from school. Ever since, he's been creeping around the corridors, taking things he needs to create his own kingdom of junk. He invites the trio to play in his imaginary palace, and while they're fine with a bit of oddness – they're at Strange Hill High – it soon becomes clear that Peter is completely mad. When Mitchell suggests they should leave, Peter won't let them go. He's been lonely for years, and now he's got some friends he intends to keep them!

Mitchell comes up with a treasure hunt game to trick Peter into retrieving all the things he stole and helping them find a way out. Delighted, Peter sets off to collect all the items on the list, ending with the "greatest treasure of all", which Mitchell says awaits him outside the gates.

And Mitchell is, by coincidence, right. What awaits Peter outside the gates is a tearful reunion with his father, who has been standing there for 100 years, hoping for his son's return. Meanwhile, Mitchell returns all the stolen items, saving himself from being expelled, even if his reputation with Abercrombie is beyond saving.

Peter's dad is still waiting at the gates!

SNOOZICAL

Becky's so exhausted she falls asleep in music class.

Auditions for the school musical are being held by mean music teacher Miss Grackle. Becky has been up all night practising, as she dreams of getting the lead part. The trouble is she's got a terrible, terrible singing voice... except when she's in the shower, or so she claims. Mitchell is not a fan of the whole idea of school musicals, and that only adds to Becky's audition anxiety.

Becky's exhausted from singing all night, so she drifts off to sleep in music class — and finds herself, Templeton and Mitchell in a weird musical dream. The school has turned into a maze based on Becky's subconscious, full of weird twists and home to a hideous monster version of Miss Grackle – the Grackle, a nightmare creature who loves music so much that she thinks it's a good idea to shoehorn "dental plaquele" into her lyrics to get a rhyme. "Dream" Mitchell deduces that they are all trapped in Becky's dream, and that The Grackle is a manifestation of Becky's anxieties.

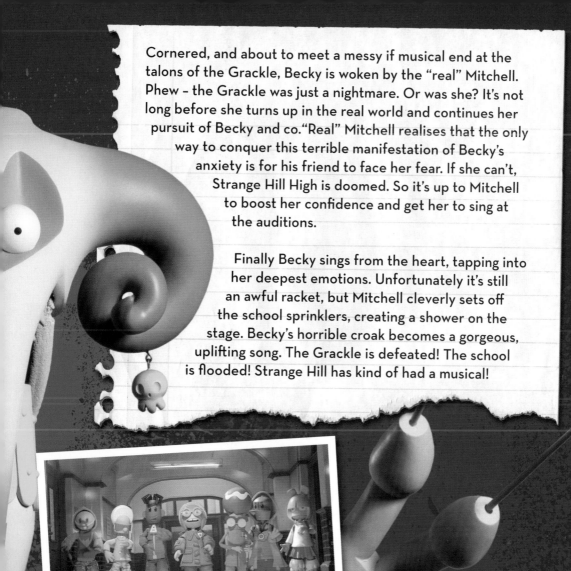

Cornered, and about to meet a messy if musical end at the talons of the Grackle, Becky is woken by the "real" Mitchell. Phew – the Grackle was just a nightmare. Or was she? It's not long before she turns up in the real world and continues her pursuit of Becky and co. "Real" Mitchell realises that the only way to conquer this terrible manifestation of Becky's anxiety is for his friend to face her fear. If she can't, Strange Hill High is doomed. So it's up to Mitchell to boost her confidence and get her to sing at the auditions.

Finally Becky sings from the heart, tapping into her deepest emotions. Unfortunately it's still an awful racket, but Mitchell cleverly sets off the school sprinklers, creating a shower on the stage. Becky's horrible croak becomes a gorgeous, uplifting song. The Grackle is defeated! The school is flooded! Strange Hill has kind of had a musical!

Becky sings "How Do You Know if You're Stuck in a Dream?" in her dream.

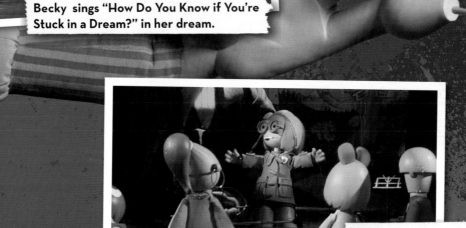

Becky sings her heart out and defeats The Grackle!

BIG MOUTH STRIKES AGAIN

Mitchell helps Becky out on the veggie snack stall.

School dinners at Strange Hill have taken a turn to the sugary side, and the kids love it. All except for Becky. She's on a health food kick and has set up a healthy food stall to persuade people to eat "sensibly". She fails miserably until she ropes in Mitchell, who invents "glo-junk" — vegetables painted neon colours. The money starts to roll in, but the school Cook is less than pleased. He steals the duo's stock, determined to destroy their business. He even sets rabbits loose on the stall.

Cook isn't normally this hostile. It turns out he's been kidnapped, and replaced with a robot! Behind this dastardly plan is the evil, cunning, ruthless (also small, pink and squeaky-voiced) Tooth Fairy! The fairy is plotting to snatch as many kids' teeth as possible so he can find the perfect tooth to finish his smilophone – a xylophone made of teeth, that looks suspiciously like a giant mouth.

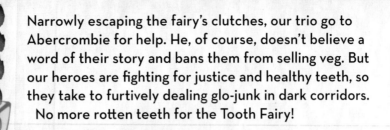

Narrowly escaping the fairy's clutches, our trio go to Abercrombie for help. He, of course, doesn't believe a word of their story and bans them from selling veg. But our heroes are fighting for justice and healthy teeth, so they take to furtively dealing glo-junk in dark corridors. No more rotten teeth for the Tooth Fairy!

The evil pink fluttery creature retaliates by kidnapping Becky, who has the perfect tooth to complete his smilophone. Taunted with sticky toffee pudding, she is unable to resist, and scoffs it down just before Mitchell and Templeton arrive to rescue her. They're too late! Becky's tooth is the final piece of the puzzle, and the smilophone is complete. It promptly eats the Tooth Fairy. He wasn't the brightest creature the trio have ever faced.

It's up to Mitchell and co to stop the smilophone from chomping the world. With the aid of a Mitchell-shaped toffee the friends lure it into gumming up its jaws, which makes it so frustrated that it explodes. And so the world is rid of the evil of the Tooth Fairy. Actually, probably not. Some monsters just keep coming back, like maths homework.

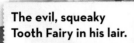

The evil, squeaky Tooth Fairy in his lair.

Nice teeth, big mouth!

THE MOST BORING BOOK IN THE WORLD

Donald is the first victim in the Library.

In the mysterious, sinister library of Strange Hill High, a boy called Donald reads from a very, very boring book. As he struggles to stay awake, a strange energy surrounds him and he vanishes into thin air. The Librarian smirks and returns the book to its shelf.

Meanwhile Mitchell and co are stuck in History when Mr Balding announces their projects are due tomorrow. Mitchell hasn't started his so he decides to go to the library to copy something out of a book.

The library? The other kids are horrified. They tell Mitchell that nobody goes there because it contains a book so dull that it bores people to death. Mitchell thinks this is nonsense and drags Templeton and Becky off to the library to help him.

Reading "A Most Intriguing History of Strange Hill High" and about to be sucked into a portal.

Mitchell nearly meets the same fate!

They find a book that seems just right. Mitchell talks his friends into copying from it while he wanders off. As soon as he's out of sight, they get sucked through a portal – a borehole in time – and deposited in the Victorian Strange Hill High. There they meet Mr Balding, who turns out to be immortal, and the author of the dangerously dull book. In the present day, Mitchell has to dodge the Librarian to find the super-boring book, which now contains messages written by Becky and Templeton trapped in the past. Mitchell goes to confront Mr Balding, but it turns out that he is not really evil, just such a boring writer that he got bored of writing his own book – but not before it created a borehole in time.

Mitchell realises the only way to cancel out the borehole is to get Mr Balding to complete his book with exciting stories. Only one thing stands in their way – the Librarian, who has been using the terrible book to warn kids away from her nice, quiet library. After an almighty battle between Mitchell and the Librarian, Mr Balding finally finishes his book. The borehole reverses, returning all the lost kids to the present day. The Librarian is beaten, the school once again has access to books... and Mitchell still hasn't done his history project.

Mr Balding struggles to think of exciting stories to write.

They're all transported back from 1881!

READ ALL ABOUT IT

The MC Bonebag concert is all sold out!

When he discovers that school newspaper "The Daily Weekly" reviews live music events, Mitchell feels a sudden urge to get involved in student journalism. It's his only chance to get tickets for the sold-out MC Bonebag gig. Unfortunately, Editor-in-chief Croydonia Puttock is no pushover. Before Mitchell gets free tickets to the gig, he has to write her a page of news, so proving that he'll be up to writing a review. But writing real news is a bit too much like homework for Mitchell, so he makes it up (like real journalists, yeah?). Becky doesn't approve, but what could go wrong?

Quite a lot, it turns out, when a Mitchell-inspired accident means that the ink drains out of the printing press and the replacement ink he finds in an ancient cupboard turns out to have magical properties. Mitchell's ridiculous news stories about a hopping virus, a plague of beards and the rugby team wearing daisy-patterned uniforms all come true as soon as they are read. And since he wrote that the school is falling apart, that's what starts happening. Murdoch is fired for failing to do his job.

Mitchell and his friends have only a few hours before the
school crumbles around their ears. They try to destroy
all the papers to stop the stories from spreading, but
Abercrombie is determined to keep some for use as
evidence against Mitchell. The only thing to do is print
another newspaper, correcting the false stories. But there
is only enough magic ink left for one copy.

Mitchell needs to think fast. He reasons that no kid
reads papers anyway – they watch TV! So Mitchell
and Templeton fake a broadcast and read the
true stories aloud, undoing the chaos. Mitchell
has saved the day. But he couldn't resist
adding a couple of extra stories, including
Abercrombie enjoying "massive rear end
results". Unfortunately for Mitchell,
the detention he gets for that one
means that he's stuck inside while
everyone else rushes out to enjoy
the results of his other additional
news story: MC Bonebag holding
a gig in the playground.

**Croydonia congratulates Mitchell
on his far-fetched news stories.**

**Murdoch the caretaker helps them
mend the broken down printer but it
runs out of ink.**

HEALTH AND SAFETY

It's Safety Week at Strange Hill High. What could possibly go wrong?

It's public safety week at Strange Hill High, so when Abercrombie slips on water Mitchell has spilt in the corridor, the trio are banished to Room 101 – the Room of Doom or, less dramatically, the audio-visual room.

Abercrombie is going to teach them a lesson they'll never forget by forcing them to watch a 1970s Health and Safety information film. It's freaky and boring, and Mitchell decides to liven things up by messing with the projector. This being Strange Hill High, he doesn't just break it, he gets himself, Becky and Templeton sucked into a 1970s version of Strange Hill High... the most dangerous school in the world. As they walk down the corridor away from Room 101, they hear the creepy old narrator start narrating them.

The friends need to escape this twisted version of their school, but with a ferocious bear lurking around every corner, the deadly threat of loose cables and even a pencil nearly proving fatal, it's easier said than done. The only way out is up.

Abercrombie introduces the 1970s Health and Safety film.

So, dodging a papier-maché head of Winston Churchill and a scissor-clutching Matthews they make it to the high ground of the clock tower.

Doom. Doom. UNSAFE, UNHEALTHY DOOM!!!

Mitchell's calls for help go unheard, and when a stray clock hand spikes up through the ground and punctures Murdoch's boiler, the entire school capsizes and turns upside down. Now the only way out is down... and up... as our intrepid trio attempt to escape to Room 101 in the basement. The film got them into this, so the film must be the way out.

With the worn-out film skipping and reversing, it looks like our trio will be stuck in the film permanently until Mitchell decides to do what he does best... break all the rules and smash the projector. Mitchell and his friends narrowly escape back to the real Strange Hill High, only to find an irate Abercrombie demanding to know why they smashed his beloved projector.

Here comes Winston Churchill's papier-maché head!

Abercrombie gets an electric shock while clearing up the broken projector.

HE GHOST WRITERS OF STRANGE HILL HIGH

Mitchell hides from Abercrombie and Mr Garden behind the trophy cabinet.

Mitchell hasn't done his homework yet again, and with his business proposal for Abercrombie's "Young Entrepreneurs" class and Mr Garden's English project on Charles Dickens due, he's desperate for somewhere to hide. A hidden passage behind the school trophy cabinet is just the ticket. It leads to a dusty old classroom that's clearly been forgotten for decades, which seems like a great hiding place until a ghost appears and asks "Are you our new teacher?" Mitchell runs for his life, leaving his homework behind.

Gathering Becky and Templeton, he returns to the secret room. There they encounter the not-so-terrifying ghosts of three Victorian children who are stuck in the "Detention of the Cursed". They've been waiting to be dismissed by their teacher for over 150 years. Not only that, but they've completed Mitchell's Dickens homework.

Hm. Three homework-completing ghost children stuck in a room? Mitchell sees his chance and puts them to work, offering a homework service to all the other kids in the school.

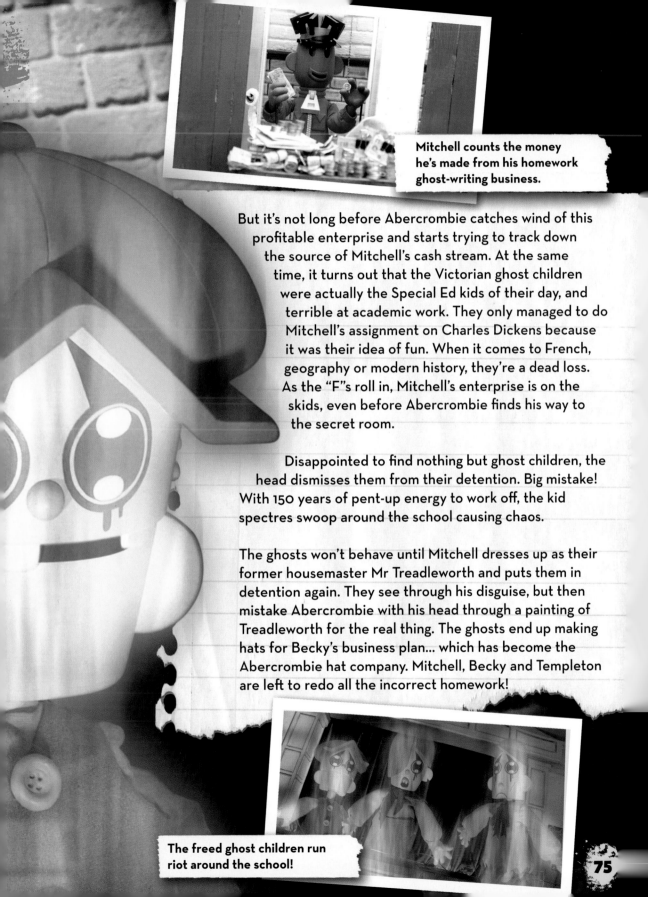

Mitchell counts the money he's made from his homework ghost-writing business.

But it's not long before Abercrombie catches wind of this profitable enterprise and starts trying to track down the source of Mitchell's cash stream. At the same time, it turns out that the Victorian ghost children were actually the Special Ed kids of their day, and terrible at academic work. They only managed to do Mitchell's assignment on Charles Dickens because it was their idea of fun. When it comes to French, geography or modern history, they're a dead loss. As the "F"s roll in, Mitchell's enterprise is on the skids, even before Abercrombie finds his way to the secret room.

Disappointed to find nothing but ghost children, the head dismisses them from their detention. Big mistake! With 150 years of pent-up energy to work off, the kid spectres swoop around the school causing chaos.

The ghosts won't behave until Mitchell dresses up as their former housemaster Mr Treadleworth and puts them in detention again. They see through his disguise, but then mistake Abercrombie with his head through a painting of Treadleworth for the real thing. The ghosts end up making hats for Becky's business plan... which has become the Abercrombie hat company. Mitchell, Becky and Templeton are left to redo all the incorrect homework!

The freed ghost children run riot around the school!

TEACHER'S PET

The Transmogrifier turns cook's potatoes into chips.

It's a snow day and with the kids having fun with snowballs, ice sculptures and chainsaws (this is Strange Hill High), it's inevitable that Mitchell and his friends will end up being sent to detention by Abercrombie. They're packed off to the science lab to tidy the place up, where they stumble across a peculiar-looking machine. It's a matter Transmogrifier, and it teleports, transforms, resizes and generally messes with ordinary objects. For example, the potato which the Cook supersizes to make enough chips for lunch.

Meanwhile, Becky has freed all the school pets from their cages on a matter of principle and Templeton thinks he's found a new deity. What could possibly go wrong? During Maths class it becomes painfully clear. What with gigantic "logs" being left around school and Murdoch being badly nibbled, it's clear that the school pets have been supersized by the Transmogrifier, and are on the rampage.

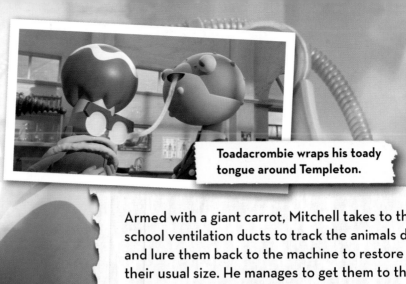

Toadacrombie wraps his toady
tongue around Templeton.

Armed with a giant carrot, Mitchell takes to the
school ventilation ducts to track the animals down
and lure them back to the machine to restore
their usual size. He manages to get them to the
science lab, but instead of turning the animals
back to normal the matter Transmogrifier hits
Abercrombie, who is carrying a toad... resulting
in the terrifying Toadacrombie: half-toad, half-
headmaster! The toad-headed head is determined
to lead his furry friends in a revolution against the
humans. The terrifying age of harmless animals
has begun!

After a battle royale that involves chainsaws, sticky
tongues and high-pitched screams, Mitchell jacks
up the power on the Transmogrifier to maximum,
causing a gigantic explosion. All the animals are
returned to normal size, Abercrombie is restored
to his previous human-ish self and Mitchell has
saved the day. All is well, even for the harmless
creatures, who have been miniaturized and
trapped in a model of the school, which they can
rule forever unchallenged.

Toadacrombie leads his furry
friends into revolution!

LUCKY BECKY

Stephanie gives Becky the job of cheer cleaner.

Becky is fed up of being unpopular and having bad luck and really, really, really wants to be part of the Strange Hill High cheerleading team. Unfortunately her audition for the team goes horribly wrong when she's responsible for the human pyramid collapsing.

Her desperation to join leads Stephanie Bethany to give her a special job... cheer cleaner. Even Becky can't be enthusiastic about picking yuck from plugholes and collecting sweaty socks, but things seemingly look up when she discovers a tatty old rabbit mascot costume at the back of the changing room. Wearing the costume, Becky gains magical powers of luck. The chess team wins for the first time and Miss Grackle's surprise test is passed by a series of fluke answers.

Now Becky is a popular centre of attention, and Mitchell realizes that having a friend who's a luck machine could mean he's on to a winner! He decides to test the powers of the costume, and when Becky wishes him luck he is immediately "spotted" by Baxter Biggs – music bigwig – who offers Mitchell stardom and riches beyond belief.

Biggs captures Becky wishing herself bad luck on camera! It's TV magic!

But there is a dark side to Becky's powers. The trio notice that all her positive actions are having an equal negative affect too. As good luck rains down, so does bad. A sweet truck crashing in the playground is soon followed by vicious zombie tigers. Becky has become a giant rabbit-shaped luck monster, and she can't break the cycle because the suit won't come off.

Thanks to the contract Mitchell signed with music impresario Baxter Biggs, Becky is obliged to wish the entire world good luck via live satellite link. Things are not looking good for the entire human race when the trio realise that Becky can escape by wishing herself bad luck. Caught in a paradox, the suit rips off her, and she's free.

So Becky goes happily back to being her unlucky, unloved self, Mitchell's music deal evaporates, and Templeton walks into a door. Normal service is restored!

BECKY VS BOCKY

Templeton demonstrates his potato-powered brainwashing machine on Mitchell.

Stephanie is standing for class president – again. But things are shaken up when Becky decides to stand against her, campaigning for green issues and the best interests of the pupils and school. Unfortunately Becky may have logic on her side, but Stephanie has shiny campaign posters which win everyone over. Templeton suggests using his potato-powered brainwashing machine to win votes, but Becky is too ethical.

Becky stages a fightback when Mr Kandinsky has everyone paint her in the art lesson. Campaign posters galore! Except for Templeton's offering, which is a horrible clay sculpture. Becky's face is going to be everywhere! Stephanie's not having that, so along with Croydonia she breaks into the art room and defaces all the pictures. But she accidentally trips the school security system, overloading the generator and shooting electricity into Templeton's sculpture. It's alive!

Stephanie uses flattery to rope Bocky into her election campaign.

Meet Bocky, Becky's biggest fan. She's also a freaky clay giant, but she admires Becky so much that Becks can't help but be won over. And Templeton has a funny turn – is he in love? Bocky becomes Becky's running mate in the election. Sadly however, what Bocky lacks in beauty she also lacks in brains, and she is soon seduced over to Stephanie's side. Now Becky is not only up against the most popular girl in school but also an exaggerated version of herself. Stephanie wins by a landslide. Did she rig the vote? It's soon revealed that love-struck Templeton has followed Bocky and defected to Stephanie's camp. He's been potato-brainwashing the whole school.

Stephanie turns potato power on Becky, trying to brainwash her, but sends a feedback loop through the school electricity system. The same electricity that bought Bocky to life sparks a big pile of trash into a monster. The monster grabs Becky but Bocky heroically sacrifices herself to save her hero.

A well-placed potato sends a surge through Bocky and the Rubbish Monster causing both to splat on the floor. Templeton is heart-broken – briefly – but turns his potato technology to good use by powering the generator. Meanwhile, Becky retires from student politics, and Cook wants to know where his potatoes have gone!

Templeton admits he's defected to Stephanie's side.

THE LOST EPISODE –
The MERCHANT OF MENACE

PLAY AT: WWW.BBC.CO.UK/CBBC/GAMES/ STRANGE-HILL-HIGH-GAME

Once you've seen the whole series, what could be cooler than a Strange Hill High game? In "The Merchant of Menace", the school is thrown into (more) chaos by the return of Elizabethan prankster Wicked William Kempe. As usual, it's Mitchell's fault, but luckily for Temps and Becks, today you're the fourth member of their gang, and you're here to save the day!

When a 400-year-old time capsule is dug up from under the school, Mitchell decides to get his homework into it somehow, so he can prove it's not late but 400 years early. Unfortunately he can't resist pressing an enticing big red button, which causes the capsule to explode and throw its contents all around the school.

When the dust settles, there stands William Kempe, the school jester from Elizabethan times. Mean headmaster Abercrombie the First locked him away in the capsule with all his pranks, which have now landed all around the school.

Elizabethan jester William Kempe... is Wicked!

Our trio escape Wicked Will on his Bloated Bilious Bladder!

Templeton uses his head to tackle Will... as a human pinball!

If Mitchell helps him retrieve the tricks, Will says he can take part in the ultimate prank, one which he's been planning for 400 years. But it's not that simple – everyone in the school has been frozen, plus Will can't resist playing a few – or more than a few – tricks on the good guys as the game progresses.

Playing the game is a chance to explore Strange Hill High yourself, moving around the school collecting useful objects (A Hairy Queen Mary Powderiser or a Spanish Inquisitor anyone?), playing mini-games and following the story as you and the gang outwit Will and Abercrombie. Just make sure you're finished by 3.30.

Mitchell and Will go head to head and rap to rap in the "Duel of Words"!

THE END OF TERMINATOR

Poor Nimrod starts to malfunction and gives out the wrong grades.

Cutting-edge technology hasn't been Strange Hill High's strength since 1862, and all the machines around the school are hopelessly out-of-date, breaking down, going up in smoke or simply falling apart. Mitchell reckons Nimrod is no better than the other disintegrating machines, and when he gets a "G" grade in a test, meaning he'll miss the school trip to an amusement park, he's determined to get revenge. He causes Nimrod's ageing and delicate circuits to fry by bombarding the teacher with illogical statements. Nimrod is scrapped and dumped in the basement.

Mr Abercrombie decides to install a risky new computerised system – it was cheap! – and along with state of the art CCTV, security systems and language lab comes a new maths teacher, the lovely Cate – Computerised, Automated, Teaching Education unit. She's a big hit with the kids and Templeton's in love again, but is she as lovely as she first seems?

Hmm, no. In fact she has an evil plan to brainwash the kids into becoming perfect obedient students. Tyson is one of Cate's first victims to be taken for re-education, and comes back polite and considerate. Weird! Becky and Mitchell realise that to take on their powerful robot foe they need a powerful robot ally. They don't have one, so Nimrod will have to do, and they go to rescue him from the basement.

Luckily Nimrod was originally designed for Cold War wargames. He's ready, willing and able - maybe - for the challenge. The kids need to act fast as Cate's zombiefication of the school is nearly complete. Nimrod strategizes that the best way to undermine an army is through their stomachs. To the canteen!

Mitchell and Becky assisted by Nimrod and his army of ageing machines unleash havoc, throwing food and milk everywhere in a gigantic food fight! Chaos trumps control and the pupils of Strange Hill join in the revolution. Nimrod and Cate go head to head. There can be only one winner... and surprisingly it's Nimrod. The school is restored to its grotty self, Cate's evil plan to take over the world is foiled and Templeton is once again thwarted in love.

A giant food fight is unleashed in the school canteen!

THE CURSE OF THE WERE-TEACHER

Mitchell is snatched by the rabid Mr Dougherty!

When Mitchell is told his career assessment has labeled him as a future teacher, he's determined to change his fate. Mr Dougherty, the mysterious and never-seen Deputy Head, is the only person who can alter the result. A search for Mr Dougherty leads the trio to the fourth floor, a previously secret and definitely sinister part of the school. The deputy head himself turns out to be a wild, hairy, fanged beast of a man who is chained up in a spooky office. Once disturbed, he pounces with his teeth bared. Mitchell is bitten by a rabid deputy head!

He manages to run to safety, but his problems aren't over yet. He isn't feeling quite himself, and keeps passing out. Meanwhile, every time a new period begins there are reports of a new and awful substitute teacher unleashing a reign of terror in the school.

Mitchell IS Mr Tanner!

It takes a while but eventually even Mitchell has to realize what the timing of his blackouts means: he has become a Were-Teacher! And worst of all, balding, grumpy, out-of-shape, disappointed-by-life Mr Tanner is Abercrombie's new best friend!

How could things possibly get worse? Well, they manage to when Mr Dougherty tells our trio that if Mr Tanner signs a permanent contract then Mitchell will be cursed to be a Were-teacher forever. On cue, Abercrombie announces a contract-signing ceremony in his office at the end of the day. The Trio must find a way to bring Mitchell back to his full-time self before it's too late.

The answer lies in the school bell: when it rings for start of period, Mitchell becomes Mr Tanner, and when end of period sounds, Mr Tanner changes back. By hijacking the bell, Templeton and Becky switch Tanner to Mitchell and back again, and back again, so fast that everyone freaks out, and Abercrombie fires Mr Tanner. The curse is broken in the nick of time... and so is Mr Abercrombie's heart.

Will Mr Tanner sign the permanent contract?

INVASION OF THE TEMPLETONS

Preparing to launch the potato-powered rocket ship...

At Strange Hill's Science Fair, Templeton has made a potato-powered rocket in order to make first contact with aliens. Unfortunately the cobbled-together spacecraft spectacularly backfires and tunnels straight down into the ground, where it uncovers an ancient flying saucer. Inside, our trio discover an alien skeleton which looks remarkably like Templeton, and accidentally reactivate the saucer, leading to a gigantic explosion. Before Abercrombie even has time to put Mitchell in detention for blowing up the playground an Alien Armada arrives and a full blown alien invasion breaks out. Typical.

The aliens turn out to look identical to Templeton, which is weird. They declare Templeton as their Supreme Being, which is even weirder. And they claim Templeton created the universe, which is possibly the weirdest thing ever.

While Templeton shows the Alien Emperor around the school, Mitchell becomes suspicious that these weird, sarcasm-immune visitors may not be all they seem.

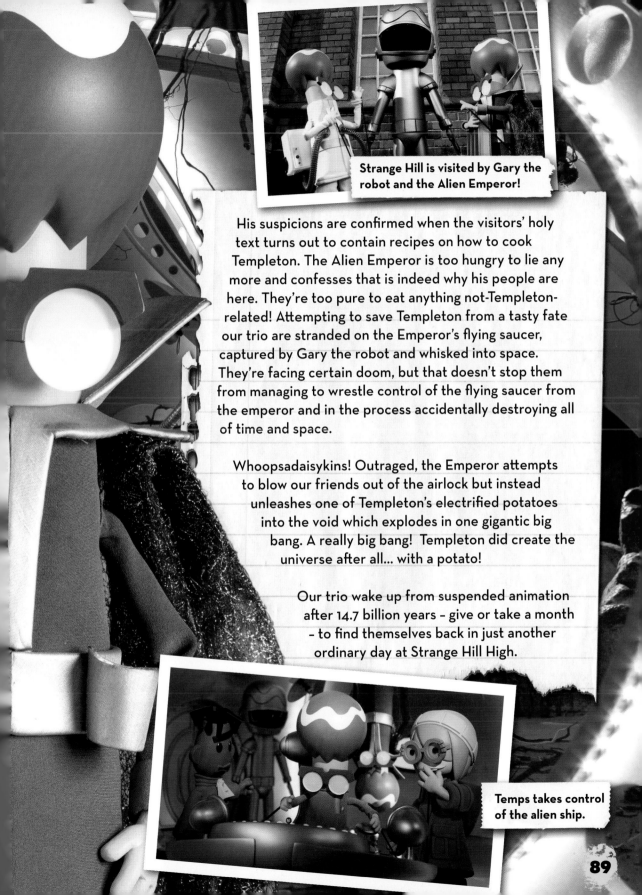

Strange Hill is visited by Gary the robot and the Alien Emperor!

His suspicions are confirmed when the visitors' holy text turns out to contain recipes on how to cook Templeton. The Alien Emperor is too hungry to lie any more and confesses that is indeed why his people are here. They're too pure to eat anything not-Templeton-related! Attempting to save Templeton from a tasty fate our trio are stranded on the Emperor's flying saucer, captured by Gary the robot and whisked into space. They're facing certain doom, but that doesn't stop them from managing to wrestle control of the flying saucer from the emperor and in the process accidentally destroying all of time and space.

Whoopsadaisykins! Outraged, the Emperor attempts to blow our friends out of the airlock but instead unleashes one of Templeton's electrified potatoes into the void which explodes in one gigantic big bang. A really big bang! Templeton did create the universe after all... with a potato!

Our trio wake up from suspended animation after 14.7 billion years – give or take a month – to find themselves back in just another ordinary day at Strange Hill High.

Temps takes control of the alien ship.

THE 101% SOLUTION

Mitchell and Templeton on a mission to steal Ian Gatlurn's 101% maths paper.

Mitchell needs 101% in the dreaded Maths "Assignment 51" or else he faces the awful fate of Summer School! Never one to let logic and sense get in the way of an easy fix, Mitchell tracks down the mythical 101% answer paper of 1950s Maths genius, Ian Gatlurn, and submits it as his own.

Unfortunately it's too much for Nimrod. He blows a fuse and Maths comes unstuck. Now one plus one equals three, Abercrombie has multiple eyes and Templeton is going bonkers (or more bonkers than usual).

In a world of broken Maths, Mitchell is a genius and soon attracts the attention of Agent Vector, a G-Man from the Ministry of Applied Mathematics. Vector's on a mission to encase the school in concrete to stop the Maths anomaly spreading. Plus he wants to confiscate Mitchell's genius brain for storage in a jar.

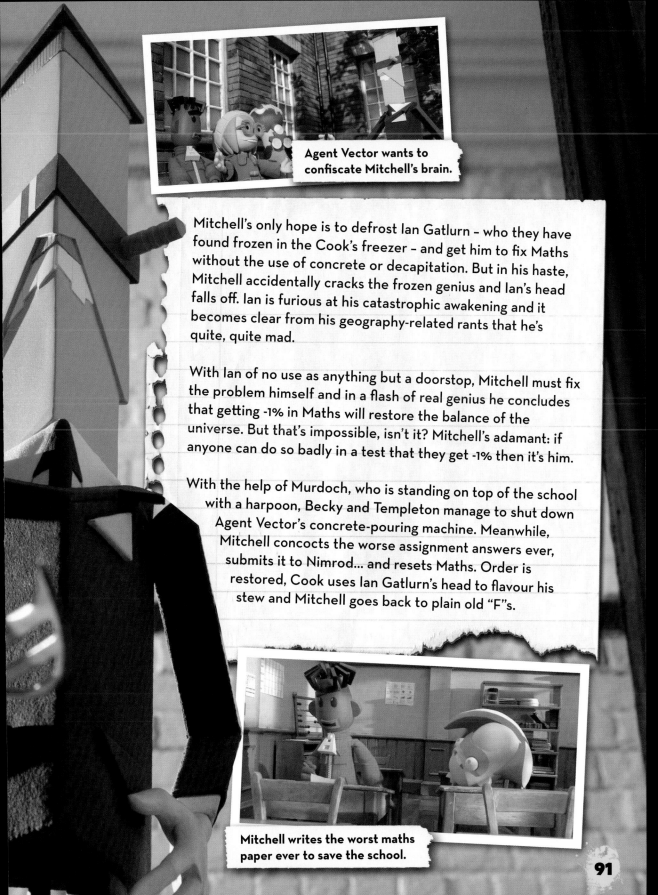

Agent Vector wants to confiscate Mitchell's brain.

Mitchell's only hope is to defrost Ian Gatlurn – who they have found frozen in the Cook's freezer – and get him to fix Maths without the use of concrete or decapitation. But in his haste, Mitchell accidentally cracks the frozen genius and Ian's head falls off. Ian is furious at his catastrophic awakening and it becomes clear from his geography-related rants that he's quite, quite mad.

With Ian of no use as anything but a doorstop, Mitchell must fix the problem himself and in a flash of real genius he concludes that getting -1% in Maths will restore the balance of the universe. But that's impossible, isn't it? Mitchell's adamant: if anyone can do so badly in a test that they get -1% then it's him.

With the help of Murdoch, who is standing on top of the school with a harpoon, Becky and Templeton manage to shut down Agent Vector's concrete-pouring machine. Meanwhile, Mitchell concocts the worse assignment answers ever, submits it to Nimrod... and resets Maths. Order is restored, Cook uses Ian Gatlurn's head to flavour his stew and Mitchell goes back to plain old "F"s.

Mitchell writes the worst maths paper ever to save the school.

LITTLE SCHOOL OF HORRORS

Inside the greenhouse the plants grow exceptionally fast!

Mitchell's plans for relaxing videogame-inspired PE lessons are ruined when Becky kicks a ball through a window. Ordered to retrieve "school property", the trio stumbles across a tumbledown greenhouse with a single green shoot surviving inside. Becky is determined to nurse the plant back to health. Mitchell is less enthusiastic, and when she forces the rest of the class to join a gardening programme, he plants a chicken nugget and fast-forwards nature with a lot of dodgy-looking extreme fertilizer.

The next day the greenhouse has unnaturally sprung into life, Becky's plant pod has burst open and a peculiar new Australian games teacher, Mr Creeper, has arrived at the school. Could the three be linked? Mitchell tries to take the moral high ground and scold Becky for creating a weird plant creature, but his authority is undermined when Jerky, a weird chicken nugget plant-animal, emerges from the greenhouse. He's like a nugget bloodhound on the trail of the creature that burst out of Becky's plant.

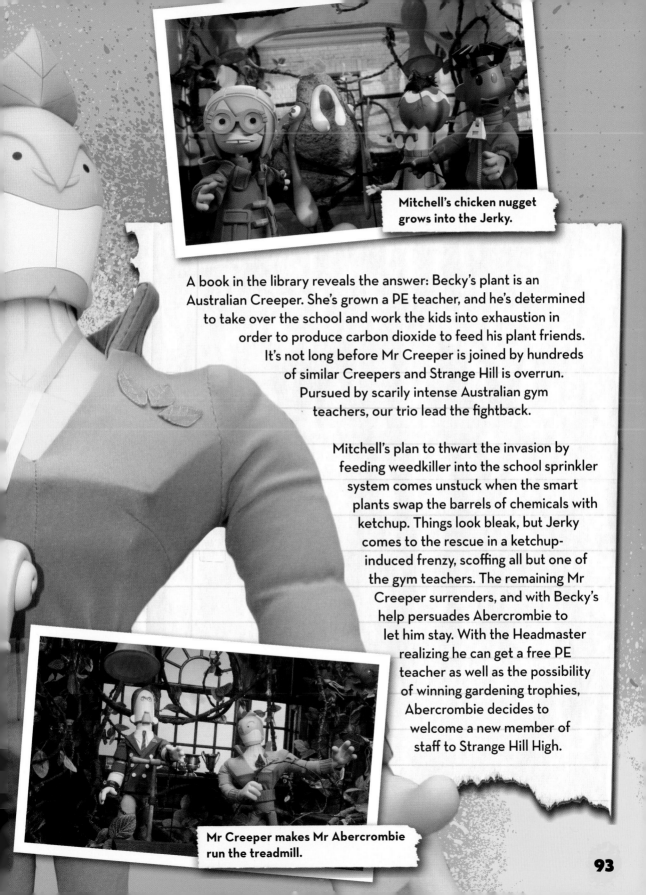

Mitchell's chicken nugget grows into the Jerky.

A book in the library reveals the answer: Becky's plant is an Australian Creeper. She's grown a PE teacher, and he's determined to take over the school and work the kids into exhaustion in order to produce carbon dioxide to feed his plant friends. It's not long before Mr Creeper is joined by hundreds of similar Creepers and Strange Hill is overrun. Pursued by scarily intense Australian gym teachers, our trio lead the fightback.

Mitchell's plan to thwart the invasion by feeding weedkiller into the school sprinkler system comes unstuck when the smart plants swap the barrels of chemicals with ketchup. Things look bleak, but Jerky comes to the rescue in a ketchup-induced frenzy, scoffing all but one of the gym teachers. The remaining Mr Creeper surrenders, and with Becky's help persuades Abercrombie to let him stay. With the Headmaster realizing he can get a free PE teacher as well as the possibility of winning gardening trophies, Abercrombie decides to welcome a new member of staff to Strange Hill High.

Mr Creeper makes Mr Abercrombie run the treadmill.

BIG TEMPLETON IS WATCHING YOU

Templeton makes the CCTV monitor room his domain.

Mitchell's new game of "footbook" causes chaos when he breaks the "prophecy" window in the library, which shows the school being destroyed by a meteor. As part of a rules crackdown, Templeton is installed as CCTV monitor and becomes the new eyes and ears of the Strange Hill High authorities. Unfortunately, power goes to Templeton's head. Not even the most minor of rule-breaking goes unpunished, making Mitchell's life a misery. Mitchell retreats to the one place the CCTV can't see, the security booth itself. He accidentally activates a strange orbiting satellite and the one CCTV monitor Templeton couldn't fix. When our trio sees themselves on the fixed monitor they realize it shows THE FUTURE!

While Mitchell sees the gift of prophecy as a chance to make a quick buck, Templeton ramps up his rule enforcement and starts detaining people for future crimes they haven't committed yet. Soon almost everyone is behind bars in the gym and Mitchell is on the run. With Gazza's help, Mitchell tricks Templeton out of his security booth and takes control of the CCTV.

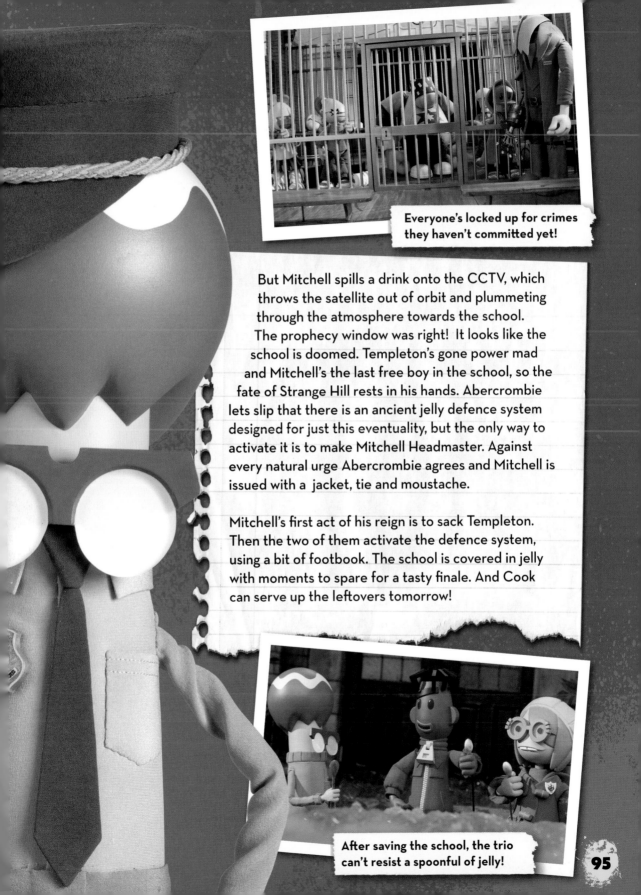

Everyone's locked up for crimes they haven't committed yet!

But Mitchell spills a drink onto the CCTV, which throws the satellite out of orbit and plummeting through the atmosphere towards the school. The prophecy window was right! It looks like the school is doomed. Templeton's gone power mad and Mitchell's the last free boy in the school, so the fate of Strange Hill rests in his hands. Abercrombie lets slip that there is an ancient jelly defence system designed for just this eventuality, but the only way to activate it is to make Mitchell Headmaster. Against every natural urge Abercrombie agrees and Mitchell is issued with a jacket, tie and moustache.

Mitchell's first act of his reign is to sack Templeton. Then the two of them activate the defence system, using a bit of footbook. The school is covered in jelly with moments to spare for a tasty finale. And Cook can serve up the leftovers tomorrow!

After saving the school, the trio can't resist a spoonful of jelly!

CRUSHING EMBARRASSMENT

It is April Fool's day and that can only mean one thing: Mitchell is pranking in overdrive. It's not long before his pranks get out of hand leaving Bishop with bolognaised trousers, Becky forced to wear a horrendously embarrassing pair of replacement glasses and a previously dormant beast of Embarrassment snatching people into a netherworld of shame.

Mitchell's in denial that he's to blame for the missing people, thinking it's part of a big practical joke, until he comes face to face with the Embarrassment. Now it's up to him and Templeton to rescue everyone, but how will they summon the Embarrassment when neither of them are able to feel shame... or are they?

A minor blunder in sci-fi trivia by Templeton is enough to throw him into a shameful tail spin and they are both dragged into the pit of Embarrassment, also known as the gym. The Embarrassment is revealed to be Mickey Barrassment, a former pupil at Strange Hill who was put into detention by Abercrombie many years previously for pranking.

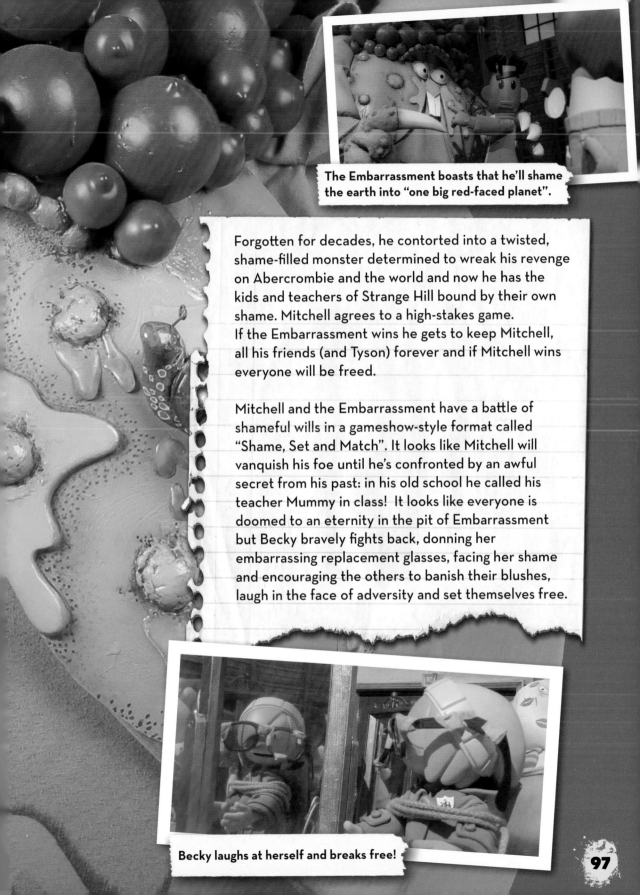

The Embarrassment boasts that he'll shame the earth into "one big red-faced planet".

Forgotten for decades, he contorted into a twisted, shame-filled monster determined to wreak his revenge on Abercrombie and the world and now he has the kids and teachers of Strange Hill bound by their own shame. Mitchell agrees to a high-stakes game. If the Embarrassment wins he gets to keep Mitchell, all his friends (and Tyson) forever and if Mitchell wins everyone will be freed.

Mitchell and the Embarrassment have a battle of shameful wills in a gameshow-style format called "Shame, Set and Match". It looks like Mitchell will vanquish his foe until he's confronted by an awful secret from his past: in his old school he called his teacher Mummy in class! It looks like everyone is doomed to an eternity in the pit of Embarrassment but Becky bravely fights back, donning her embarrassing replacement glasses, facing her shame and encouraging the others to banish their blushes, laugh in the face of adversity and set themselves free.

Becky laughs at herself and breaks free!

MITCHELL WHO?

The monsters are back!

Mitchell has got more "F"s than Becky has ever seen. Any more, and he faces suspension! He could improve his grades through hardwork and diligence but nah, he'd much prefer to erase his results from the school computer. Aided by Templeton he lures Miss Grimshaw out of her booth, then sets about deleting his grades on the Victorian steam-powered computer. Patience is a virtue, one which Mitchell lacks, so he rashly deletes his entire record. Success! Total and complete success. In fact, not only does nobody remember his grades, they've also forgotten him.

The Grackle grabs Becky!

Mitchell takes advantage of the situation to annoy Abercrombie and snatch sausages, but when even his friends fail to remember him and his body is starting to disappear, it's obvious that things are serious. Not only that but Strange Hill itself seems to have changed. Mr Garden is Headmaster, Templeton is head bully with Tyson, Lucas and Bishop as henchmen, and Becky is terribly lonely and talking to imaginary friends.

Samia is the only person with any recollection of Mitchell, as she has a short-term memory built into her personal computer. Even worse, all the villains and monsters Mitchell's ever defeated, including the Tooth Fairy and the Grackle, are back! Mitchell persuades Samia to help him – for a fee – and the two of them try to restore Mitchell's identity by reinstalling his school record in the ancient database. Entering a strange, primitive, digital world, Mitchell and Samia speed around, narrowly avoiding the strange velocipede defences. Moments before Mitchell disappears forever, he is restored.

But the monsters are still on the rampage! Why? Because Mitchell didn't just vanquish all those bad guys himself. Templeton and Becky were there too. Mitchell gets the gang back together and in the nick of time order is restored, the bad guys disappear and Strange Hill is back to normal... except Mitchell still needs to delete his "F"s. Luckily, just this once, Samia offers to do it for free.

Samia helps restore Mitchell's identity on the ancient database.

INNERCROMBIE

It's Valentine's Day and Mr Abercrombie is stamping down hard on any smushy wushy, blubbery flubbery romantic nonsense. Anyone doing anything romantic is instantly in detention. Mitchell grasps this golden heart-shaped opportunity, and by incriminating all the staff in romance ends up with a teacher-free school. While attempting to top off his trick by filling Abercrombie's office with Valentine's stuff, Mitchell and his friends are trapped and hide in a cabinet. The cabinet turns out to be a sticky portal to the inside of Abercrombie's head.

The kids have their very own drivable headmaster with working voice box, and Mitchell monetizes the situation selling tickets for the Attack of the 100ft Headmaster ride. Becky's determined to treat Abercrombie like a human being but not before having a bit of fun at his expense.

The Headmaster is starting to get worn out, and bursts into tears! The trio are almost drowned in blubbing, deafened by a rusty heart and blasted with the steam of rage, but that's nothing compared to the problems caused when the bullies take control of their headmaster. Mitchell and his friends must regain the upper hand before Strange Hill High is bullied into submission. Becky's always believed the heart rules the head and now's her chance to prove it. Mitchell plays along with this "hippy-dippy nonsense" and lures the bully-powered Abercrombie to the library.

Becky's plan to pump up Abercrombie's heart by sneakily encouraging the Librarian to quote romantic poetry seems to go well, and the bullies bail out of Abercrombie's head to escape the mush. Unfortunately that leaves Abercrombie driverless and in full-on romantic mode... He only comes to his senses when the Librarian says he can stay in the school with her forever. Love may be blind but it's not stupid, and Abercrombie comes to his senses, frees the teachers from detention and ends his affair. Things are back to normal at Strange Hill High, not that you can really see much of a difference.

Our trio find themselves staring out of Abercrombie's eyes!

Inside Abercrombie's head, Becky attempts to take the controls from bully Tyson.

KEN KONG

"Wow! A tropical island paradise!"

The day starts well with woodwork: the only class without rules. Mitchell and Templeton both make aeroplanes. The difference is that Templeton's is big enough to actually fly in. When Abercrombie announces a surprise swimming assessment, Mitchell flushes all the swimming costumes down the toilet. But his plan is sunk when ridiculous Victorian swimsuits are issued and the kids are forced to jump into the freezing cold pool and swim a very lengthy length.

When it looks like no one can go on, a tropical island paradise emerges from the fog and the swimmers are washed up on its sandy beach. Mitchell claims the island as "Mitchelltopia: land without rules". Unfortunately, someone else has got here first. No sooner do the kids relax than they hear a terrifying roar. Obviously (if you are Templeton) it comes from the Island Beast And/Or God And/Or Experiment Gone Wrong, and the kids must make a sacrifice to it.

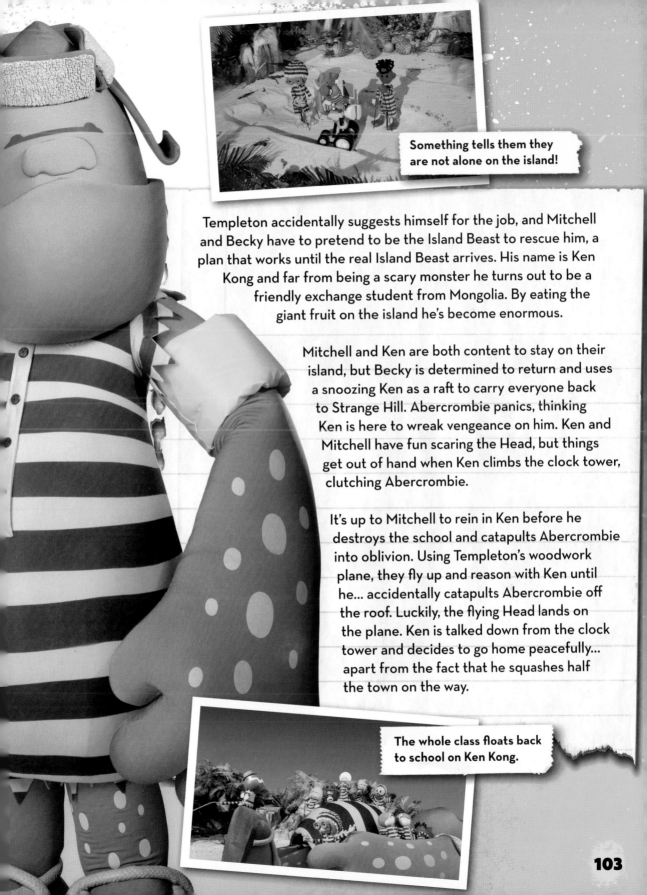

Something tells them they are not alone on the island!

Templeton accidentally suggests himself for the job, and Mitchell and Becky have to pretend to be the Island Beast to rescue him, a plan that works until the real Island Beast arrives. His name is Ken Kong and far from being a scary monster he turns out to be a friendly exchange student from Mongolia. By eating the giant fruit on the island he's become enormous.

Mitchell and Ken are both content to stay on their island, but Becky is determined to return and uses a snoozing Ken as a raft to carry everyone back to Strange Hill. Abercrombie panics, thinking Ken is here to wreak vengeance on him. Ken and Mitchell have fun scaring the Head, but things get out of hand when Ken climbs the clock tower, clutching Abercrombie.

It's up to Mitchell to rein in Ken before he destroys the school and catapults Abercrombie into oblivion. Using Templeton's woodwork plane, they fly up and reason with Ken until he... accidentally catapults Abercrombie off the roof. Luckily, the flying Head lands on the plane. Ken is talked down from the clock tower and decides to go home peacefully... apart from the fact that he squashes half the town on the way.

The whole class floats back to school on Ken Kong.

MITCHELL JUNIOR

Lunchtime for the trio and their babies.

With the death of Mr Stingles, the class pet wasp, Mr Garden is convinced it's time the kids learned about responsibility. He issues everyone a "baby" but Mitchell is late for class so he gets the last doll in the box... and it's the evilest ventriloquist dummy you ever saw!

While baby-related havoc breaks out, Mitchell tries to ditch his doll. But no matter where he puts it, it mysteriously returns. Meanwhile, Mr Abercrombie is on a binge of new Choc-o-splosion bars, Templeton is proving to be a brilliant parent whilst Becky's doll is coming apart at the seams due to neglect. Mitchell finally reaches the end of his tether and whips out the clockwork power source of his doll. That should be the end of it but no, the doll turns to him and asks "Why did you do that, Daddy?"

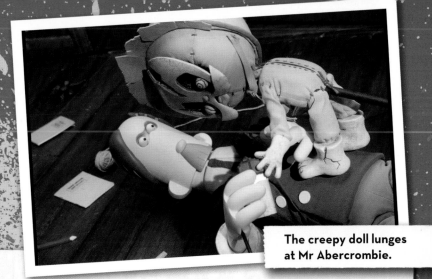

The creepy doll lunges at Mr Abercrombie.

Mitchell is sent to Mr Abercrombie's office to explain his disruptive behaviour but while there the doll comes to life and steals all of Abercrombie's Choc-o-splosion stash. Maybe this strange "baby" isn't so bad? Mitchell and Mitchell Junior have some fun playing pranks until Junior crosses the line in pursuit of chocolate and gets into a full-blown tussle with Abercrombie. The doll turns on Mitchell, and as they struggle it falls into the school recycling pit. Is this the end of Mitchell Junior?

Guilt-ridden Mitchell enlists his friends to rescue his doll from the recycling machinery but the trio end up trapped themselves in a rubbish compactor and facing certain doom. In the nick of time Mitchell Junior comes to the rescue, scooping up all the other simulation dolls and dumping them in the machinery. The works grind to a halt, our trio is safe, Mitchell has learned responsibility by destroying things and Mitchell Junior has gone to a better place... He's in Abercrombie's office scoffing chocolate.

Mr Abercrombie and the doll become a chocolate-loving duo.

THE MCDXX MEN

Ratman, Iron Maiden and The Leech in the ancient chamber.

Mitchell is so obsessed with his latest handheld game that he collides with Mr Abercrombie while skateboarding down the corridor. The Head is thrown through a door and into a rage. He immediately confiscates all electronic devices in the school and locks them in the basement. Determined to get down to the basement and reclaim his game, Mitchell persuades his friends to join him in the dodgy abandoned elevator. Unfortunately it breaks, and crashes into a long-forgotten cave. The cave turns out to be the ancient headquarters of Ye Olde Righteousness League – a trio of medieval superheroes who long ago fought an evil super-villain, the Rapscallion.

Donning the medieval super-hero costumes, Mitchell becomes Ratman, Becky is Iron Maiden and Templeton takes on the sucking abilities of The Leech. They will fight tyranny... and get Mitchell's game back!

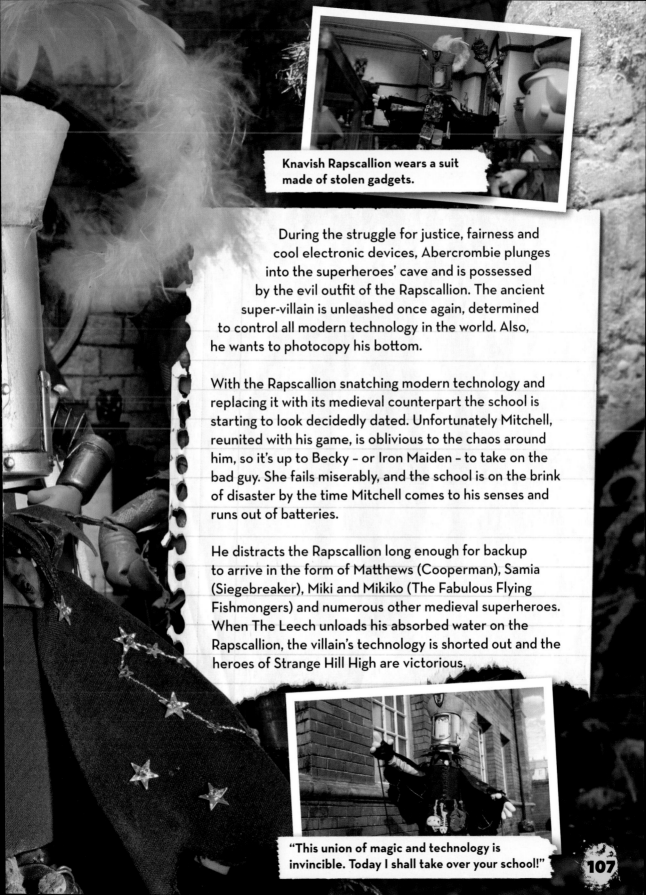

Knavish Rapscallion wears a suit made of stolen gadgets.

During the struggle for justice, fairness and cool electronic devices, Abercrombie plunges into the superheroes' cave and is possessed by the evil outfit of the Rapscallion. The ancient super-villain is unleashed once again, determined to control all modern technology in the world. Also, he wants to photocopy his bottom.

With the Rapscallion snatching modern technology and replacing it with its medieval counterpart the school is starting to look decidedly dated. Unfortunately Mitchell, reunited with his game, is oblivious to the chaos around him, so it's up to Becky – or Iron Maiden – to take on the bad guy. She fails miserably, and the school is on the brink of disaster by the time Mitchell comes to his senses and runs out of batteries.

He distracts the Rapscallion long enough for backup to arrive in the form of Matthews (Cooperman), Samia (Siegebreaker), Miki and Mikiko (The Fabulous Flying Fishmongers) and numerous other medieval superheroes. When The Leech unloads his absorbed water on the Rapscallion, the villain's technology is shorted out and the heroes of Strange Hill High are victorious.

"This union of magic and technology is invincible. Today I shall take over your school!"

THE SNIDE PIPER

Miss Joy and her class singing in perfect harmony.

It's time to celebrate the Spring Festival by singing and playing merry tunes. Unfortunately the kids are so amazingly terrible at it that their horrible efforts send Miss Grackle running out of the school, swearing never to return. Abercrombie'll be needing a supply teacher, then. But before he can even complete the necessary phone call, Miss Joy turns up.

She's beautiful, a touch mysterious, and vibrating with, well, joy. There's something weird going on – happiness at Strange Hill is just unnatural. With Joy on the case, there's a sudden outbreak of near-talent in the class. And there's also a sinister mini-Stonehenge rising from the playground, but nobody notices that yet.

Mitchell, Becky and Pepé, the French exchange student standing in for Templeton, notice something's a bit off and back out of music class. Meanwhile, the other kids are brainwashed, and skip out of the classroom after Miss Joy. Everyone's wearing hippy robes – including Pepé once Miss Joy gets him. Mitchell and Becky take refuge in Mr Balding's office, and the old history teacher tells them that Miss Joy is actually Terpsichore, a goddess who is here to join her world to ours… by sacrificing Mitchell. She ends up chasing the three of them down the corridor.

Things are looking bleak when Mitchell and Becky run into Matthews, who is horrendously cheerful like the rest of the brainwashed kids. But this is a different horrendous cheerfulness. A built-in one. Mitchell realizes that Matthews is impervious to Joy because of his ridiculous natural happiness. It's time for MC Mitchell T to form a band out of his new crew: Bex in Effex, Mild Master Matt and DJ Baldy Baldman. They pit their individuality rap against Joy's songs of harmony, but their forces are evenly matched – until Joy uses her secret weapon, the brainwashed and beautiful-voiced Pepé.

Joy is about to prevail, when Templeton comes back and sings more horribly than anything yet. It's so horrible that Miss Joy's vortex shorts out, then sucks her in and vanishes. Templeton forgot his passport. Or Abercrombie forgot to give it to him. Either way, the regular Templeton AND a French version are complaining to Abercrombie…

Mitchell and the crew rap up a chorus!

A STRANGE HILL HIGH CHRISTMAS

Templeton and Mitchell find explosive Tudor crackers in the Lost and Found.

Mitchell is desperate to go on his Christmas holidays early, so when he learns of a school board rule stating the building has to be closed if the temperature falls below a certain level, he sabotages the boiler. Unfortunately he's a bit too successful, as the entire school freezes solid, trapping everyone inside. All attempts at escape are foiled, so it looks like Christmas is cancelled. Staff and pupils are all furious. Even cheerful old Mr Balding is strangely unhappy and acting suspiciously.

Becky is determined to make the best of the situation and goes into festive overdrive. As Mr Balding is the most unhappy, he is her main target for an assault of Christmas "good cheer". Under constant badgering, Mr Balding confesses that he doesn't like Christmas because he lost out on becoming Santa Claus to one of his classmates at school. But could he be lying?

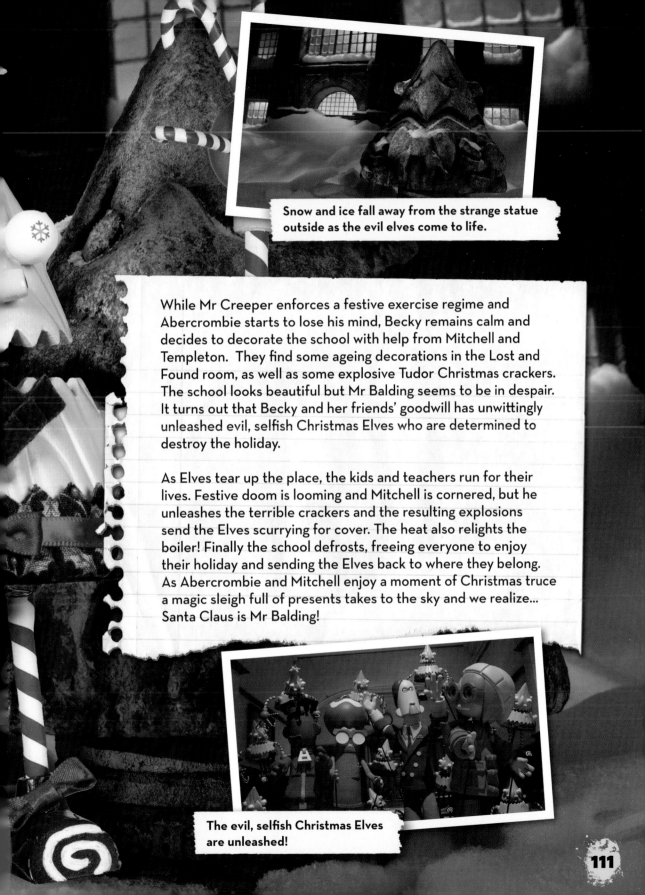

Snow and ice fall away from the strange statue outside as the evil elves come to life.

While Mr Creeper enforces a festive exercise regime and Abercrombie starts to lose his mind, Becky remains calm and decides to decorate the school with help from Mitchell and Templeton. They find some ageing decorations in the Lost and Found room, as well as some explosive Tudor Christmas crackers. The school looks beautiful but Mr Balding seems to be in despair. It turns out that Becky and her friends' goodwill has unwittingly unleashed evil, selfish Christmas Elves who are determined to destroy the holiday.

As Elves tear up the place, the kids and teachers run for their lives. Festive doom is looming and Mitchell is cornered, but he unleashes the terrible crackers and the resulting explosions send the Elves scurrying for cover. The heat also relights the boiler! Finally the school defrosts, freeing everyone to enjoy their holiday and sending the Elves back to where they belong. As Abercrombie and Mitchell enjoy a moment of Christmas truce a magic sleigh full of presents takes to the sky and we realize... Santa Claus is Mr Balding!

The evil, selfish Christmas Elves are unleashed!

CHARACTER QUOTES

Most of Strange Hill is quoteable. Here are some of the bzest:

"Everything's normal. No-one's learning anything."

"Whassup? Somebody **EXPLODE?**"

"Action beats study"

"Solve it with science and **schemes**"

"Initiating **panic** phase"

"All _dreams_ are illogical"

"I'm a very needy person"

"Brainwashing's not ethical!"

"This is clearly a very bad thing."

"That'll be **five pounds**."

"E*wwwww*!"

"You ain't the king of bling! That's my thing!"

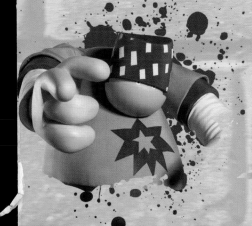

"I WOULD RATHER NOT BECOME INVOLVED IN THIS MATTER."

BEHIND THE SCENES

On set, working the puppets.

Manoeuvring the props into position...

Filming the favourite trio...

BEHIND THE SCENES:

Interview with the Showrunner:

Josh Weinstein

The showrunner of **Strange Hill High** is Josh Weinstein, who was previously a writer on the American animated show **The Simpsons**.

"Being the showrunner means I serve as lead writer but also supervise all other aspects of the show. That could be designs of new characters, storyboards before we film it, the music that goes with each episode, etc. I'm often in the United States, and our show is filmed in Manchester, UK, so I see a lot of designs, footage etc over the internet. But nothing beats actually being on the sets as they film the show!

Strange Hill High is my very favourite thing I've ever done. It's so different and strange and it's never been done before, yet it's made so well – anything we come up with in our twisted imaginations, our team is able to make a reality. It's like playing in the greatest miniature world ever.

Growing up, I spent a lot of time reading comic books and watching cartoons. Then I realized "Hey, wait a minute! Somebody actually writes those things! I want to do that!" Breaking into professional writing was a bumpy road for a while, but at **The Simpsons** I found a lot of like-minded weirdos. Now at Strange Hill High I have a whole new group of friends who also enjoy thinking up and making really weird, funny stuff! "

Before it's filmed, each script of Strange Hill High is drawn as a long cartoon strip, known as a storyboard. This shows the directors and puppeteers how the writers intend the story to look, and helps everyone spot any mistakes, such as over-long scenes, before filming starts.

Part of the storyboard from **The Curse of the Were-Teacher**, written by Josh Weinstein.

BEHIND THE SCENES:
Writers

Andrew Burrell

Each script goes through many stages before being filmed. First a draft is written by the main scriptwriters (the people whose names you see on the credits at the start of the show). Then it's reviewed by several other writers. They'll all have suggestions, and by the time the script's been discussed it may need to go through a rewrite... or five or ten. Work doesn't stop until every line is as funny as possible. Script Editor Andrew Burrell oversees the process.

 We always have a story that starts with something quite ordinary which spirals out of control in a weird, Strange Hill way. We like surprising twists, freaky monsters, funny jokes and our trio heroically fixing the problems that they (Mitchell!) have usually caused.

It can take more than six months to write a single episode of **Strange Hill High** – from coming up with the original idea, until the script is ready to film. No idea is too silly for our show, but what it's really about is three friends having a good time.

When the writers get together to make up stories we spend most of the day laughing. We all understand that our trio may be made of vinyl but they think and act like real – but hilarious – kids. My main job as script editor is to work with the head writer Josh to make sure that the adventures are both cool and funny.

I was rubbish at school, so getting to work on **Strange Hill High** was really down to a lot of hard work and a lot of luck. It helps that I watched too much TV as a kid and I always enjoyed writing. 🙶

Like all TV scripts, **Strange Hill High** episodes have to be laid out in a particular way. Each scene is numbered (1 in the picture) and so is every line (for example, 6 in the picture).

1

1

EXT. SCHOOL - ROUND THE BACK - DAY

ROMANTIC MUSIC swells as we SOFT FOCUS on MURDOCH, up a ladder, staring directly at us with a ~~~~ of flowers as an arm attachment.

MURDOCH
Shall I compare thee to a s~~ day? Thou art more full of ~~ and more metallic. Beside~ can't kiss a summer's day.

1

Murdoch looms towards us for a kiss... ~~ ~~. Just as generator. She's covered in hearts and roses. Murdoch's lips are about to make contact, the **TANNOY** screeches into life blasting a **YELPING** Murdoch out of frame.

ABERCROMBIE (OVER TANNOY)   2
Attention! Valentine's Day is
hereby banned at Strange Hill High.

A battered and bruised Murdoch comes into frame covered in rose petals with his bunch of flowers now a withered stump.

2

MURDOCH   3
(woozy)
Love hurts.

3

ABERCROMBIE (OVER TANNOY)   4
I'm stamping down hard...

4

2

INT. ABERCROMBIE'S OFFICE - CONTINUOUS

While holding the Tannoy mic, Abercrombie is trying to stamp down on a heart-shaped balloon but, to his great frustration, it keeps flooping out from under his foot.

2

ABERCROMBIE
...on any kind of lovey dovey...

This is part of the script from **InnerCrombie,** written by Andrew Burrell.

5

3

INT. MR GARDEN'S CLASSROOM - CONTINUOUS

The Tannoy blasts as Becky clutches a Valentine's Card with "Mr G" written on it in her handwriting.

ABERCROMBIE (OVER TANNOY)
...smushy wushy, blubbery flubbery
nonsense.

6

6

BECKY
You can't ban Valentine's Day. You
might as well ban feelings!

7

7

Abercrombie appears right behind her holding the Tannoy mic.

BeHIND THe SceNes:
Puppeteers

Strange Hill High has an unmistakable look, and much of that is down to the amazing puppets, and the skilled people who bring them to life. Made from vinyl, they're completely different from the puppets used in other shows. They're also very expensive – each one is worth thousands! Tim Jones is one of **Strange Hill High**'s puppeteers.

Tim Jones

Being a puppeteer is a bit like being a wizard, except you don't have to have a beard (and cloaks are fairly impractical). A puppeteer turns an inanimate object into a living, breathing, believable character with all the energy and motivations of a real emotional creature.

Strange Hill High mixes traditional rod-puppets with computer-generated effects, which I love. The puppets are beautiful, with some ingenious mechanics inside. They bring their own special challenges because they are very small and the camera is often very close. This means that every tiny movement appears much bigger on screen so we have to work within just a few millimetres. We also have to wear eye protection, hard hats and dust masks sometimes, because of all the props, jelly and slime that get thrown around the set.

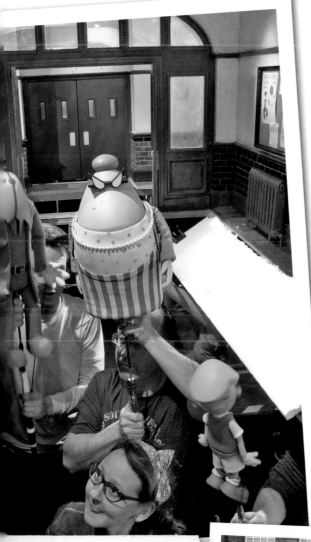

It can sometimes take three or four puppeteers to get a character to move the way you want it to: someone on the head and body, someone else on the hands, another on the legs and a fourth puppeteer might be flapping their clothes or moving a prop. In one monster-heavy scene, we had twenty people under the set!

The voices have already been recorded so we puppeteer to the audio being played out of speakers in the studio. It's very satisfying being able to add even more to the performance by puppeteering what we hear, as well as inventing body-language for what we can't.

The puppeteer team have to work meticulously within a small space under the set.

It takes many camera people and puppeteers to film a small scene showing the outside of the school.

BEHIND THE SCENES:
Art and Animation

A lot of work goes into making a puppet-based show. Every single thing you see on the screen has to be made by hand, to an incredible level of detail. Barbara Biddulph is art director for **Strange Hill High**.

Barbara Biddulph

 There are a lot of stages to go through in creating a show like **Strange Hill High**. As art director, I visited old Victorian buildings and photographed walls, radiators, pipes and architecture. That helped us to get the feel and textures right for an old, forgotten school.

Set design was a challenge, because we need to have access below for the puppet rods, so all the floors have to be removable, as do the walls so the camera can get in. It takes a huge team of very skilled people to build all this.

As well as sets, I oversee the prop build. We need everything from exploding science experiments to dodos dressed as Rudolph the Red-nosed Reindeer. Once we get shooting, the art department team are in the studio dressing all the sets as they come in. If something doesn't work or isn't quite right for the shot which the director sets up, we change it, and quickly! This can be extremely stressful if your glue won't stick and there are six people watching you.

Each day brings many challenges – how can we get Murdoch to jump out of a cake? Answer: thin polystyrene sheet painted to look like icing and perforated so it breaks in a controlled way. How do we make green slime? Answer: 100 pints of green jelly piled on the set. That's a lot of jelly.

Sounds fun? It is.

The set of the library.

Covering the set with green jelly for the **Big Templeton is Watching You** episode!

BEHIND THE SCENES:
Voice Actors

Doc Brown

The first part of Strange Hill to be recorded is actually the voices. Then the animation and puppet work is created to go with the audio track. Doc Brown is the voice of Mitchell.

"My favourite thing about Mitchell Tanner is his name. It's the kind of cool name I wanted as a kid! He's by no means perfect, but he's massively loyal to his friends and would risk his own wellbeing for them. I think he's a little hero with some little flaws and a big heart.

Mitchell finds himself in all sorts of trouble. Robots, psychotic fairytale characters, the future, giant guinea pigs... It's too varied to pinpoint any one thing – Strange Hill is a troublesome school.

It's been amazing working with Josh Weinstein. He's very clear with his vision for the show so he's easy to respect and take advice and inspiration from. Plus he's got that experience of writing on **The Simpsons**.

I think what visually makes Strange Hill stand out is that it looks like such an original mix of retro and the future in terms of puppetry mixed with the incredible FX. It's basically like horror – I find it quite creepy at times, and mixed with the savvy comic writing it makes the complete package just something else!"

Emma Kennedy is the voice of Becky.

" Becky Butters is an overly optimistic underachiever. She's hopeless at everything but never gives up. Hope always springs eternal for Becky.

What I really like about her is how she's neither pretty nor especially clever. She's un-extraordinary in every way. What she has is boundless enthusiasm. She's like the runt of the litter but at her core is a loyal, decent girl who is willing to stick up for her pals and do the right thing. I admire her resilience and her determination, the way she doesn't let failure get her down. She's a fighter. And I think the lesson she can teach is that you may be small but you can always be determined.

The best thing about **Strange Hill High** is the sense of energy and fun. I love the puppets, the sets are incredible and the storylines are incredibly inventive. "

Emma Kennedy

Richard Ayoade

Richard Ayoade is the voice of Templeton.

THE LAST WORD

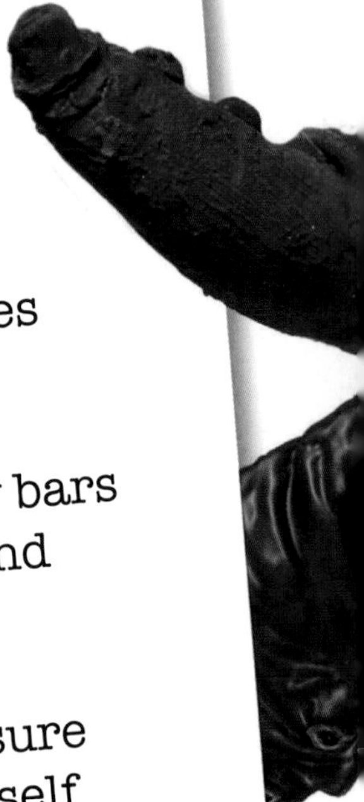

I hope that this modest introduction to our establishment of learning has helped you feel that Strange Hill High is the place for you or your child to enjoy a top-quality education, free from bear attacks, hauntings, consumption by aliens or other inconveniences which DO NOT HAPPEN HERE.

Either way, there are 200 Chocolate Insanity bars waiting for me in my office, so just go away and leave me alone.

I would like to take this opportunity to reassure you of the professionalism and values of myself and my entire pedagogical team.

Kind (of) regards,

Abercrombie

Melvyn Abercrombie
**BA (Honest),
Basingstoke Stereo
Salesmen's College**

Did you know there is an entire race of aliens out there who worship me? It mostly just means they want to eat me, which is illogical, because Tyson is a lot bigger. But I suppose if you imitated Tyson you wouldn't be good at spaceship science. I'm special. I always knew I was special. I was born for great things, like Dimtrona of Thargh, who knew not of her destiny as a child, but grew up to become Overlady of the Frites Galaxy. Except I'm a boy so obviously I won't be an Overlady, I'll be an Overape because the Lord of the Apes bade me.

Becky says this isn't what I'm supposed to be writing about. She doesn't know that the evil cupboards are plotting to take over the classroom, and this is an encoded secret message begging for help from the good and noble blackboard people. Oh no, I've given it away!

Templeton

We really hope you've enjoyed reading this book, which is all about Strange Hill High. If you've gone mad or been eaten or anything, then I really, sincerely apologise, because that is the sort of thing that happens around here and you just have to go with the flow and not get too uptight. I try not to get uptight, but wouldn't you if you got a C instead of an A in Geography because your teacher turned into a demon horse that could do hoofprint Cs but not anything else, and your homework got eaten by a three-headed dog from the underworld ... oh dear, it's just all a bit much.

But stay positive! It all works out in the end, until we die horribly.

Love,

Becky

According to my mum, I always have to have the last word because I'm a smartmouth. Well yeah. So here we go:

BONEBAG
CHKA CHKA CHK-A- CHK-A-
CHK-A- CHK-A
BONEBAG

Word!

Mitchell